Ministry
of the
Dispossessed

Ministry
of the
Dispossessed

**Learning from the
Farm Worker Movement**

Pat Hoffman

WALLACE PRESS
Los Angeles

Published by Wallace Press
Los Angeles, California

ISBN: 0-941181-00-6

Library of Congress Cataloging in Publication Data: 86-51483

Hoffman, Pat
   Ministry of the Dispossessed
   Bibliography: p. Index
   1. Ministry.   2. Church and social movements.
   3. Organizing as ministry.   4. Liberation theology.

Printed in the United States of America

To Mendota, California and the farm workers who worried, worked and suffered there. You taught me some of my most important lessons.

Table of Contents

Foreword

Way back in the beginning of our Union, someone asked what we expected from the Church. I answered that we did not want more churches or cathedrals; rather, we wanted the Church to be present with us, beside us, willing to sacrifice for justice, ready to be Christ among us.

At the time, I wasn't thinking about how much the farm workers in the union—the strikers and the boycotters—were themselves the Church-in-the-world, showing the way for many Christians who yearned for a better world. We were not, of course, trying to make a theological statement. We were just doing what we had to do for the sake of a measure of justice in the fields. And, as it turned out, many thousands of people from the churches joined us along the way.

The Migrant Ministry led from the beginning. They were beside us with support and with their lives. I am sure they had their anxious moments, but it did not keep them from throwing themselves into the middle of our fight. And from that position alongside us, they pulled significant parts of the non-farm worker Church into our movement.

Pat Hoffman has done a remarkable job of telling the story of the Church's involvement with the farm workers union. Even more importantly, she has demonstrated through the experiences of individuals, how participation in the UFW struggle challenged people's values and priorities, shaped their understanding of social change and led them in directions that truly changed their lives.

These determined farm worker supporters then affected the priorities of the Church by forcing the agenda of the poor into meetings and assemblies and public worship in ways that most of us in the Union did not fully appreciate at the time.

The challange of the Union's struggle also changed the lives of farm workers, forcing them to make hard decisions about their basic economic security and placing the issues of justice and future hope for their children, in the center of family life.

Many workers and spouses and children made sacrifices for their cause that are still an inspiration: going on strike with little or no resources in reserve, and traveling to strange, cold, far-away cities to tell the story of the strike and boycott to any person or any group who would listen. In almost every case, those sacrifices for justice brought remarkable human growth, a deepening of religious faith, and an unshakeable confidence in the unifying power of non-violent struggle.

As the churches face new challenges and controversies in communities of the poor all over the world, it would be wise to reflect on the lessons learned by the Migrant Ministry's pilgrimage in the fields. I know that farm workers will never forget the people who stood with us in those darkest days when no one believed that a farm worker's union could survive and actually bring about change. And it is also hard to forget those others who turned their backs on us when the need was greatest.

Our struggle for justice in the fields continues. The poor in many places call on the Church to risk comfort and privilege for the sake of God's peace and justice. Pat Hoffman's book is not only clear and readable and historically important, it also points the way for the Church to learn from the poor and to gain spiritual life and strength from the movements of the dispossessed.

Cesar Chavez, President
United Farm Workers of America, AFL-CIO
La Paz, Keene, California

Acknowledgments

This book was Fred Eyster's idea. Fred is the Co-Director of the National Farm Worker Ministry. His idea became a reality because he was willing to search for grant money to help cover the expenses of writing the book. Special thanks to Harvey and Lois Baker of Florida and our friends in the denominations for their help in that regard.

Thanks go to my husband, Cecil, whose courageous decision to go to Mendota, California, set my life on a path with people in struggle. He read and discussed the ideas in the book and forthrightly advised me on what would express the story well. He also revealed the mysteries of computer technology to me as I needed new revelations.

Many people consented to be interviewed for this book. I love their stories and treasure the insights and experiences they shared with me. Not every person interviewed is quoted in the book. But every person's insights helped form the ideas expressed here. All those interviewed are listed in the Bibliography. There must be hundreds of people I would have liked to interview. Practically every friend I have was significantly involved with the farm worker movement. I was overwhelmed with the task of deciding who *not* to interview.

I interviewed people who represented categories of folks who had been involved: students, farm workers, clergy, middle-class, middle-aged church people, denominational executives, Migrant Ministry staff, Church Women United, and UFW or former UFW staff. There is special attention paid to the United Church of Christ, which, of all the denominations, took the most heat for their support of the farm workers.

Of those interviewed, three deserve special note. Jim Drake had a singular role in the involvement of the Church with the United Farm Workers Union. He made a long car trip in order to meet me in San Antonio, Texas, and then submitted to an entire day of interrogation and taping. After all that, he and his wife were gracious enough to take me to dinner. He gave me several excellent ideas for approaching the material. I've tried to use them.

Chris Hartmire was the Director of the Migrant Ministry (later called the National Farm Worker Ministry) during the years examined in this book. While I have been writing the book, he has had major responsibilities with the United Farm Workers. But he cheerfully gave me enormous amounts of time for in-person interviews, numerous phone conversations, painstaking review of the manuscript to find details I had gotten wrong or missed, and encouragement. And he and his wife, Jane, provided a place for me to stay when I would travel to La Paz.

Cesar Chavez worked me into his demanding schedule more than once. But more important than the interviews has been his leadership with farm workers and the opportunities his style of leadership has given to the middle-class Church.

I'm grateful to Winthrop Yinger for trustingly lending me his excellent collection of primary documents. I hope Fresno State University will be able to find the duplicates which were given to them.

Besides Cecil Hoffman and Chris Hartmire, the manuscript has been read by Chris Glaser, an outstanding Christian leader and valued friend, and by Dr. Roland Tapp, a distinguished church educator and editor. For those of us who write, our manuscripts are our babies. We entrust them only to the best.

Introduction

IN THE EARLY SIXTIES and seventies the tiny California Migrant Ministry led thousands of middle class Christians into involvement with a movement of dispossessed people, farm workers, from whom we learned about faith, courage, empowerment, and non-violent change.

What can movements of dispossessed people bring to the Church that is energizing and renewing? What do the poor encounter when they try to get help from the institutional Church? How can people and structures help or hinder involvement?

This book explores the lasting imprint of farm workers on the lives of some of their supporters and on the Church. And it examines the prophetic witness of the Migrant Ministry, an ecumenical agent of the Church, in putting the risky requirements of the poor first.

My own involvement with farm workers began when I was twenty-three years old. It was 1958 and my husband Cecil and our two babies moved to Mendota, California, in the central agricultural valley of that State. Cecil was fresh out of seminary. Neither of us wanted to return to the suburban church kind of situation we had grown up in. Cecil was to be part of the California Migrant Ministry's (CMM) rural fringe ministry to workers settling on the outskirts of towns and cities in the Valley.

This was before farm workers started organizing under the leadership of Cesar Chavez. Their poverty shocked me. The inhuman treatment they routinely received angered me. But so few people really cared, a few church people, the American Friends

Service Committee, a newspaper man named George Ballis in Fresno, we could name the advocates of farm workers, list them on a sheet of paper. We worked hard for improvements for farm labor, but seldom had a victory of any kind.

Our family left Mendota in 1961 and moved to Los Angeles. That same year Rev. Wayne "Chris" Hartmire was hired as the Director of the CMM. He and his family came to Los Angeles, where the CMM had its office. He was our continuing link with events among farm workers. I was many miles away from farm workers geographically. But in my mind and heart I had not left.

I was excited when Chris Hartmire told me in September 1965 that the workers had gone on strike in the grape growing area of Delano. If there was to be any change it had to start with farm workers. They were the only ones who consistently, day after day, felt the burden of conditions as they were. If their anger, their determination could be mobilized, there was a chance for change. Could Chavez give them enough hope to try? Could I, a homemaker with three little children, help in some way to contribute to their hope?

Before the month was over, I took the task of phoning pastors for donations of food for the strikers. When the strike stabilized as a strong, on-going event, Sue Miner in the CMM office started calling me to speak to church women's groups interpreting the strike and later the boycotts. In 1970 I began part-time, paid work with the CMM. I was full-time on the staff in 1971 when the National Farm Worker Ministry was formed.

But it is easier to say what I did than what happened to me. And what happened to me happened to many. I was organizing church people to help the farm workers and I saw that other supporters felt as I did, more empowered, more alive, more hopeful because of their contact with the farm worker movement. What happened to supporters in the decade of 1965 to 1975, and how it happened, and what the lasting impact has been, is what this book is about.

I want these stories to contribute to the continuing faithfulness of the Church to the poor and dispossessed, especially when the poor are on the move, creating the conditions for justice. No individual Christian or congregation should be deprived of the means of grace which involvement with the poor in struggle can provide.

I have limited the scope of this book to experiences in the Christian community. Jews were significantly involved, as well as other faith communities, in the farm worker movement. I have concentrated on what I was most familiar with.

CHAPTER 1

Early Ties Between Church and Farm Workers

I had long before thought through and learned that in order to achieve social justice you have to try to match power with power. As long as the farm workers were not organized, they had no way to stand up to the growers and request and win increases in salary and working conditions.

Dr. Walter Press

THE DC9 ROLLED TO A STOP under the outside lights of the St. Louis airport terminal. The ninety-five passengers were running on pure adrenalin. They had been in meetings all day and through the evening, but now they felt hyped for the flight to California. Some of the more committed felt a catch of emotion in their throats. The outside terminal door was opened and their charter flight was announced.

They walked out of the terminal into the muggy summer night air, and up the portable stairs into the plane. Some were remembering the prayer for them, "O God, we send from our midst our fellow members of this General Synod to represent us among our brothers and sisters who are suffering injustice in Southern California . . . Bless, protect and defend them."

There were a few minutes of crowding into the plane, people with their carry-on luggage for the twenty-four hour trip, stowing bags, looking for seats and seat mates. The leaders were running lists in their minds of everything that had to be taken care of: monitors, instructions on non-violence, information about arrival plans in California and when they would be returning to St. Louis, rejoining the Ninth General Synod meeting of the United Church of Christ.

Within a few minutes everyone was settled and the plane taxied down the runway and, with a surge of the engines, took off flying west. It would have been a good time to catch a few winks but it was hard not to think about facing the Teamster hired "goons" who were waiting in Southern California's Coachella Valley. Everything had been so predictable until two days ago, on the very first day of the Synod meeting, when delegate Jan Beilly announced from the floor that the Teamsters had "unleashed a campaign of violence against the farm workers on strike in Coachella and Arvin." Cesar Chavez, President of the United Farm Workers Union, had personally phoned and asked for a small delegation of observers to come to Coachella and witness what was happening. But so many delegates wanted to go that this DC9 had to be chartered to carry them all.

Rushing through the night on this plane to join a violent scene in California seemed unreal. There were second thoughts. Especially the people who were only coming as observers, who hadn't been involved in the farm worker struggle through the last eight years. How were these "goons" to know the difference? A sign saying, "Don't club me, I'm just an observer"?

The full story of what happened to the United Church of Christ delegates comes later in the book. But they did return to St. Louis the next night changed people.[1]

In the 1960's and '70's virtually every major religious body in the United States and many in Europe and Canada gave attention to U.S. farm workers, took positions on what the workers were doing, and were a significant force in rallying 17 million Americans to participate in the common act of not buying grapes.

Yet there were only two million farm workers in the country. And of that small number, most were poor, uneducated, many did not speak English, most were not registered to vote, in fact, might not even have a home address, and were scattered across the nation. But in 1962 a farm worker turned organizer left a good job in the city because he felt called to right some injustices among farm workers. His name was Cesar Chavez and he started a small association of farm workers which first was called the National Farm Workers Association (NFWA). The members of that association managed to engage the interest, resources, and commitment of national and international Church bodies. And, as a result, revitalized the spirits of thousands in and out of churches. How did the Church get so involved with this marginal group of America's migrant workers? And how did the Church and the NFWA become the elements for a rare vintage? This book will give the formula for that classic vintage. The major elements are never quite the same from one year to the next. But the formula is priceless.

To understand we have to go back a few years.

CHURCH WOMEN GET ORGANIZED TO HELP

It must have been a shock to Edith Lowry the first time she visited a migrant camp. Lowry would become the moving force for women's work among migrants. But that first time would have been distinctive, driving out one of the typical back roads, past verdant fields, to arrive at a ramshackle camp of tiny one-room shacks, whole families living in each one. And the people she met. The broken-down young men and women who had been raised in the migrant stream and never could get enough money to get out. They grew up in these camps, married and had babies, and

the babies grew up riding from camp to camp and field to field—
if they didn't die in infancy.

On the first trip everything that Edith Lowry had heard about
migrants became real in the people she met. A woman about her
age explained about the camp. Her voice was flat and tired. It was
evening and she pointed out her father sitting on a broken step
of a nearby shack. He looked twenty years older than his sixty
years. "He won't be able to stop working 'til he dies," she said.
Her youngest child was shyly hanging behind her skirt. The two
older girls had devised some sort of game with sticks outside.
They were all clearly malnourished.

Four day care centers had been started by the Council of
Women for Home Missions in New Jersey, Maryland and Dela-
ware in 1920. The wrenching poverty of migrants drove Edith
Lowry to expand the work of the Council of Women. By 1939
she had opened programs for migrants in fifteen states. From the
work of the Council of Women for Home Missions came regional, local, and state Migrant Ministries related to the National
Council of Churches, which was formed in 1950. For more than
thirty years the Church concentrated on giving direct aid, child
care, educational programs for children and adults, summer recre-
ation, and worship opportunites in these isolated migrant camps.
Church women's organizations around the country sent health
kits for migrants and pooled money and coupons to purchase
"Harvesters", station wagons equipped for staff to take the
educational and religious programs out to labor camps.[2] Farm
workers appreciated the help. It was all that could be done at the
time. But some Migrant Ministry personnel were asking questions.
Why are farm workers so poor when their work is crucial to keeping a nation fed? Why didn't conditions improve for agricultural
workers as they did for industrial workers? What keeps these
dreadful conditions from changing?

By the 1940's the labor movement had jarred loose thousands
of industrial workers from poverty and poor work conditions. But
labor unions had been frustrated in their many attempts to bring

the benefits of organization to farm workers. Among the reasons for their failure was the specific exclusion of farm labor from the National Labor Relations Act passed in 1935 to protect workers trying to unionize.

A later significant barrier to organization was the passage of Public Law 78, the Bracero Law, under which large growers could order up a given number of Mexican workers from the government. The workers were cheap and easily controlled. When the harvest was over, they were sent home. PL78 was passed by Congress in 1951, during the Korean War with the manpower crunch as a pretext. It continued until 1964. The easy availability of "braceros" undercut the economic effectiveness of strikes, and forced domestic workers to compete with a large, docile pool of imported workers. No effective organizing could be done until the Bracero Law was ended.

CALIFORNIA MIGRANT MINISTRY
GETS INTO ORGANIZING

Doug and Hannah Still came to work for the Migrant Ministry in Kern County in the central valley in 1950. They were teachers. Their major assignment was to get the school system committed to educating migrant children. You might ask, "Isn't that what schools are supposed to do—educate children?" Yes, of course. But it has been a complex problem to educate migrating children, and an educating job to get a community school system committed to that responsibility.

Here's a typical conversation that Doug and Hannah would have had with the school authorities in Kern County in 1950.
Hannah: We're glad to meet with you, Mr. White, as superintendent of schools. We have just completed an extensive survey of migrant children in the school district, with the total number of children, what week their families usually arrive in Kern County in the Fall and when the family usually leaves in the

Spring. We have also noted the number of school age children who were not in school at the time of our survey and for what reasons.

Mr. White: I can see you've gone to a great deal of trouble getting all this information. You're new here, aren't you?

Doug: We moved here six months ago. We're teachers employed by the Migrant Ministry to work with migrant children.

Mr. White: We think it's wonderful the way the Migrant Ministry people get out to the camps and put on programs for migrants.

Doug: Mr. White, you're probably aware that here in California farm labor are migrating less. They do often arrive in Kern County after school has started in September. But many migrant children are in the area most of the school year.

Hannah: Many of them don't show up at school because they don't have shoes or are ashamed of their clothing. But we want to propose some ways the school system could better meet the needs of migrant children.

Mr. White: Mrs. Still, before you go any further, you should know a few things about our schools here. I know you and your husband mean well and want to help these unfortunate children. But this County has had migrants for many years. Traveling is a way of life for these people. It's a care-free way of life. They have no mortgage payments to worry about, no yard to keep up. They take no responsibility in the communities they pass through. And they pay no taxes. Our schools are paid for by the people who live here. Those are the people who join the PTA, who take an interest in the schools and in their children's education.

Doug: Are you suggesting that migrants aren't interested in their children's education?

Mr. White: They have a different way of life. Frankly, the children don't need much education to pick beans and dig potatoes.

Hannah: Mr. White, migrants are as interested as you and I in their children's education. They want them to go to school so they can get out of the migrant stream.

Doug: This country has assumed an obligation to provide public education for all children regardless of how poor their families are.

Mr. White: We have many migrant children in our schools. Any child may be enrolled in the schools.

Doug: But the fact is many migrant children are not in school. They are illegally working in the fields with the full knowledge of growers and foremen. And many are home caring for younger brothers and sisters. And the schools are doing nothing to see that these children get to classes.

Mr. White: During September and October our class sizes are twice what they ought to be because of all the migrant children. We are not going to take responsibility to drive out to all these camps and fields trying to find more children. If their parents are so concerned about their education, they can see to it that they get to school.

Hannah: What we want to propose are some ways to handle the uneven class sizes you referred to, and let migrant families know the schools care and are interested in educating their children.

Mr. White: Our school system doesn't have the money to institute new programs for families who pay no taxes. We're doing the best we can. If the Church is so concerned about migrant children, they should keep the camp educational programs going. Most of these children will never be able to fit into a regular school program. They usually are two or three grades behind for their age. It makes it very difficult for the teachers.

The Stills had many such "deadly conversations." They had no success in impacting the school system. The Rev. Doug Still recently recalled, "None of the people-serving systems wanted to serve migrants."

After two and a half frustrating years, Doug Still decided to leave for awhile to prepare himself to empower migrants. He observed that the only institution which had an interest in farm workers was the Church, but felt that non-ordained people had little clout. So he decided to go to Union Theological Seminary in New York City and concurrently to study community organization at the New York School of Social Work. His seminary thesis was on community organization as mission, using farm workers as the specific focus.

Although Still was on leave from his work with migrants, he and Velma Shotwell, Western Area Supervisor with the NCC's Division of Home Missions, stayed in touch while Still was in New York. During his three years at seminary, he regularly attended meetings of the National Council of Churches' Division of Home Missions, CMM's parent body. He got to know denominational leaders and talked up the idea of denominations setting up rural fringe ministries in California to serve farm workers who were settling in rural slums. By the time he finished seminary and was returning to California as the director of the new California Migrant Ministry (CMM), several denominational leaders were ready to start rural fringe ministries.[3]

During Still's last year in New York, the Rev. Dean Collins, who succeeded Shotwell with the Division of Home Missions, was taking steps to give community organizing training to CMM staff so they could help farm workers build power. The focus of the CMM was on seasonal farm workers who had partially left the migrant stream to settle in the many shanty towns up and down the central valley of California. The CMM was interested in organizing these newly settled people to identify community problems which there was some hope of solving, such as getting curbs and gutters, fire protection, and uncontaminated water.

The staff knew that the basic problems were related to wages and working conditions, but the CMM at that time "had no intention of taking on labor issues," seeing nothing but "defeat for farm workers in a direct labor confrontation with their employers."[4] The Agricultural Workers Organizing Committee, AFL-CIO (AWOC) was working in several areas of California and CMM staff were interested and supportive.

In February 1957, Dean Collins met with organizer/trainer par excellence, Saul Alinsky, of the Industrial Areas Foundation. With them in the meeting was an innovative organizer from

California named Fred Ross. Ross had extensive experience with farm workers and had developed a Latino organization called the Community Service Organization (CSO). The three men came up with a plan to train Migrant Ministry staff in organizing techniques. The program was to be financed by a grant from the Schwarzhaupt Foundation.

When Doug Still got back to California as the Director of the California Migrant Ministry, the plan went into gear. Over a three year period CMM's staff and board got organizing training with Fred Ross or Cesar Chavez of the CSO.[5]

Doug Still was CMM director for less than four years. But during that time he built a staff committed to self-determination for farm workers. He also brought to fruition several rural fringe ministries, denominationally funded and administered, but with the CMM providing consulting and supervisory services to staff. These ministries in their original design had three components: pastoral ministry, community organization, and social service for farm workers who were settling.

Mendota, California, population 2500, was the first town to get a rural fringe ministry. Mendota is nearly in the middle of the great central agricultural valley, thirty-three miles northwest of Fresno. In 1958 the town itself was mostly whites and Hispanics hanging on by their fingernails to middle class status. The rural fringe was an unincorporated area that looked like part of town, but it wasn't. The Southern Pacific railroad tracks made a wide—about six tracks wide—barrier between unincorporated East Mendota and those people hanging by their fingernails west of the tracks in Mendota.

When you crossed the tracks to the east, the paving ended giving way to rutted dirt streets and abandoned cars. No sewer lines connected to the shacks which had recently been moved there after being condemned on ranch property. There had been a little crack-down by the State Department of Health and some of the growers decided it was too expensive to fix up their camps. Instead, they sold the shacks to farm workers and had them moved to the edge of Mendota, Tranquility, Firebaugh and other towns up and down the central valley. The shacks were no better for the move.

Most of the residents of East Mendota were black farm workers. It was a point of pride for ladies in Mendota, especially those in Bonnie Heights—the section where people no longer hung by their fingernails to middle class status, they had already achieved it—to brag, usually with a trace of Southern drawl, that, "I have never been in East Mendota." The whole town with both its parts was so small, so lacking in entertaining, or even pleasant features, that it's a wonder ladies didn't slip clandestinely into East Mendota just from curiosity.

The few rich people were mostly growers living out from town on their ranches. Many of them had once been poor themselves, immigrants or dust bowl refugees. They had worked hard and gotten rich. They said that anyone with gumption could make it as they had. But conditions had changed from the thirties and forties. They didn't know it, or didn't want to know it.

I moved there with my husband, Cecil, and our two little ones in the blistering summer of 1958. Doug Still had hired Cecil just out of seminary. We were tired of stuffy suburbs and jumped at the chance to go to Mendota where Cecil pioneered rural fringe ministry. He was to be pastor of the Mendota Methodist Church (which is no longer in existence), with part of his salary coming from the Methodist Church and part from the Migrant Ministry. In the Fall of 1958, Paul Ashton was hired to be the community organizer on the team.

Paul was black, a member of the conservative Church of God, and very committed to his new job. He was living in Fresno, thirty-three miles away. But after working all week he would travel back to Mendota Sunday mornings to attend our tiny Mendota Methodist church service.

The idea of the rural fringe ministry was to bring the ministry of local congregations to farm workers who had moved from outlying labor camps into the shack communities on the edge of towns. Paul and Cecil were trying to do that by bringing that little congregation into contact with farm workers in East Mendota and in the camps, and by inviting farm workers to participate in worship and programs of the congregation.

Ladies who drawl, "I have never been in East Mendota," find a black Migrant Minister difficult. A few weeks after Paul started the job, the church secretary's husband (he was director of the church school), phoned Cecil to tell him they were quitting the church. His wife was getting nauseated every Sunday from having to sit in church with a black man.

Their leaving was the opening salvo in status quo versus change in the rural fringe ministry. In Mendota it was followed by an angry refusal by the women of the congregation to continue preparing monthly church potlucks because a hungry—white—farm worker family ate too much. And it escalated into larger battles with angry community people calling the Methodist congregation "the farm worker church", though only a few farm workers attended. Later there would be spirited exchanges about meetings held in the Ministry's community building in East Mendota for labor organizing.

Mendota illustrates from the grass roots the entrenched racism, the clinging to status, the desire to identify with the few who were the growers and were rich. These were rural communities with well-installed power structures. Everybody knew everybody, and they weren't about to change so a bunch of damned farm workers—fruit tramps—could get some of the goodies.

The confrontations didn't stay in these little communities. Denominational staff in Los Angeles and San Francisco drew heat from local communities for these rural fringe ministries. Denominational executives had to understand the projects, and be committed to self-help and self-determination for farm workers in order to answer accusations.

The Rev. Wayne (Chris) Hartmire came as director of the CMM in September 1961. He was a twenty-nine year old with round blue eyes and white teeth that had never required orthodonture. When Jane Eichner, his future wife, and other girls visited

Princeton on the weekends they thought he was very good looking. Some might have been surprised that by twenty-eight he was married with a family, living in East Harlem and working in the East Harlem Protestant Parish. Hardly the kind of achievement they might have expected from a bright engineering student. In the service of his ready compassion, his brain works like a high-powered computer, all the time sorting, prioritizing, storing. He applied his mind equally to engineering and faith. He soaked up what they had to offer at Union Seminary in New York and came out knowing the Bible like a Baptist and with the social ethics of a Presbyterian—which he is.

East Harlem was a good bridge between seminary and California's migrants. It prepared him for the racism and its consequences. And East Harlem had taught him, he says, about the "dignity, worth, wisdom, and survival strength of the Black and Puerto Rican poor."

So he brought to California his wife Jane, three cute kids (a fourth was born in California), astonishing energy, and a commitment to farm workers being organized on their own behalf. Through Hartmire's twenty year stint as director, he would see remarkable fruits of self-determination for workers like the weary women Edith Lowry met.

HOW THE LINKS WITH
THE FARM WORKERS UNION DEVELOPED

In his definitive 1967 paper, "The Church and the Emerging Farm Worker Movement," Hartmire points out that the fight to end the Bracero program prepared the ground for more controversial actions later on. The churches played a significant role in pressuring Congress to end PL78, and the CMM was at the center of it. Between 1961 and 1964 there was a raging controversy in California as the "forces that opposed the mass importation of farm labor seemed to be gaining ground." Hartmire comments that the bracero fight "prepared us psychologically for conflict." It also narrowed the base of financial support, which Hartmire considered positive, as it committed the CMM to resources less dependent on a program of ameliorative services. This would prove useful in the years to come.[6]

Several more rural fringe ministries developed in California in the early sixties, at the prodding of the CMM. One of these was most closely associated with the Ministry's moving from organizing for community development to direct involvement with the farm workers' union.

Dr. Richard Norberg was new in 1960. He had been called to the top position, Conference Minister, of the Northern California Conference of the United Church of Christ. And the UCC was a new denomination, formed in 1957 from the Congregational Church and the Evangelical and Reform Church. His Conference was called Northern California, but it included the San Joaquin Valley stretching 300 miles up the center of the State. A number of the former Evangelical Reform churches were in the Valley.

Norberg picked as his Associate Minister a man from the Evangelical Reform tradition, but less conservative than many. In fact, his Associate Minister, the Rev. Walter Press, was deeply committed to social justice.

The two of them spent days traveling up and down the San Joaquin Valley getting acquainted with all the pastors and the congregations and the conditions of life in their far-flung Conference. As they traveled they saw the "countless number of shack communities", the rural fringes. The evident poverty and suffering concerned them. The UCC's already gave money to the Migrant Ministry for work among migrants. But in 1962 Norberg and Press got interested in the idea of their denomination having a rural fringe ministry in cooperation with the Migrant Ministry. With the solid cooperation of Dr. Shirley Greene, of the national UCC staff, they decided to start a project in the small community of Goshen, just north of Delano.[7]

They notified Chris Hartmire that they wanted to start a rural fringe ministry in Goshen. Would he keep his eyes open for a staff person? Hartmire had heard about Jim Drake, who had just finished his studies at Union Seminary in New York. Drake was a Presbyterian from the little farming community of Thermal, California, in the southern agricultural area called the Coachella Valley.

Drake was looking for a position where he could combine outdoor work with his ministry. He's a big man, well over six feet tall, and solid like the Republican Party he had voted for two years before when he turned twenty-one. He had come from a "conservative mold politically," according to Drake, "but pietistically caring." Now he was twenty-three and married. He was on the verge of taking a job as a chaplain with the National Parks when Hartmire reached him at a cabin in the Sierra Mountains.

Drake went to Goshen to meet with Hartmire and to discuss the job. Hartmire explained the terms of the position and told Drake that he would be doing community development. So this rather conservative, solid young man accepted the job and then went to the library to find out what community development was. The library offered little help. So, not knowing exactly what it was he was supposed to do, he asked permission to spend some time just getting acquainted in the community.

Goshen was just another little unincorporated burg straddling Highway 99. You might get off the road at Goshen if you were having car trouble. There were several gas stations, even more liquor stores, a small church with a steeple, little wood frame houses with some struggling zinnias, a few hollyhocks, and prickly pear cactus. Everything looked in a state of sun stroke.

Soon after Drake started work in Goshen, Chris Hartmire phoned and told him that an important CSO organizer, Cesar Chavez, was leaving the CSO and moving to Delano to organize farm workers. Hartmire wanted Drake to have training with Chavez. He arranged for Drake to accompany him for a month, driving Chavez around in Drake's car, using a CMM gas credit card. Drake recalled his first impressions of Cesar, "I watched the guy and I knew he was nuts because he was going to do this big thing."

Drake learned a couple of political lessons quickly after taking the job in Goshen. Soon after he started with the CMM, he drove to his home presbytery[8] to make arrangements for his ordination. He was "dumbfounded, hurt and angry" to discover that Riverside Presbytery would not ordain him. They did not consider his work with the CMM to be a "call". This was straight politics reflecting the negative attitude in California's agricultural areas toward organizing farm workers for self-determination.

Drake phoned Walter Press of the UCC Conference and asked if the UCC would ordain him. Press said yes. Drake was ordained by the United Church of Christ in December 1962. The pain and rejection that he experienced when his own denomination would not ordain him did not dissipate for years. It was mirrored by the anger and rejection felt by members of his home congregation in Coachella who were so dismayed by his decision to be part of the CMM that some demanded the return of a set of *The Interpreter's Bible* they had given Drake in seminary.

Drake and his wife, Susan, got settled in Goshen and started getting to know people, most of them farm workers, and problems in the community. The Goshen people wanted to get street lights and have some streets paved. Drake took these requests before the County Board of Supervisors. "They would mutter and scoff, and laugh. And I would go back, and I could never understand why nothing was happening. I was just beginning to experience powerlessness from the Goshen point of view . . . I did not want to stand in front of the Board of Supervisors anymore if I was not going to win, because I did not like the idea of people snickering about the people in Goshen."

In the meantime, Drake was setting up house-meetings for Cesar Chavez's cousin, Manuel, who was traveling to different communities trying to get members for the new National Farm Workers Association (NFWA). Drake still thought that the NFWA was "a dream world."

The UCC was trying to figure out what a rural fringe ministry should look like in Goshen. They decided to build a community center. They acquired a piece of land and some funds and with the help of work projects from city churches got it built. Drake liked the idea at the outset because it was a concrete task. But by the time the center was built, he felt he had made a mistake, and that he would end up being a youth director at the center.

How could the CMM help the people of Goshen and other farm workers achieve some degree of self-determination? How could the Ministry serve the poor in this situation? Drake and the Migrant Ministry began conceptualizing a county-wide organizing project which would begin in one area and eventually build a "coalition of people's organizations that would change the political shape of the County."

The Rev. Phil Farnham, Drake's former classmate at Union Seminary, was brought in to direct the Goshen Community Center. Toward the end of 1963, Jim Drake and Gilbert Padilla, who had been with the CSO, opened "a tiny little office in Porterville" (40 miles north and east of Delano). By this time, the NFWA, Chavez's organization, had grown and had some things to offer in farm worker communities. They were publishing a low-cost magazine called *El Malcriado*, "the voice of the farm worker," and Drake was writing articles for it. And the NFWA offered farm workers death benefit insurance, and membership in a co-op that sold retread tires and motor oil at discount prices. Organization for farm workers was building now in several places.[9]

By 1964 the CMM put together its resources with some from the UCC and the Rosenberg Foundation to hire a third staff person, the Rev. David Havens, who had had training with Cesar. The Tulare County Community Development (TCCD) project was formed.

The Tulare County field staff focused their organizing efforts on low income Mexican-Americans, most of whom were seasonal farm workers. They started an organization called the Farm

Workers Organization (FWO). Hartmire in his 1967 paper explains, "Membership in the FWO was limited to farm workers so that middle-class Mexicans and Anglos could not join and dominate the organization." Dues were set at $2.00 per month. "Our hope was to develop a self-supporting coalition of organizations across the county in two years." The FWO worked on "the bracero issue, voter registration, development of low income housing, unfair or illegal rents, individual wage claims, welfare issues." Also they started a small gasoline co-op with about 100 families.[10]

Jim and Susan Drake moved from Goshen to Porterville and joined the Congregational Church there. A man named Jim Hazen was pastor. He had no way of knowing the worry and turmoil that was about to take over his ministry. "We turned his life upside down in a period of about six months . . . He was a real nice guy caught in the middle of all this stuff."

SUGAR BEETS TURN THE CHURCH SOUR

The first substantive issue the Tulare County project got involved in was wages in sugar beets. There was a federal minimum wage of $1.40 for sugar beets because it was a subsidized crop. But no sugar beet workers in the area were getting that wage. They were being paid piece-rate, and many children were working on their parents' social security cards. People were actually getting about 70 cents an hour.

The first case was of 80 workers at the farm of one of the "top dogs in the Porterville church." "We dragged him into court. It wasn't forty-eight hours before Walter (Press, the UCC Associate Executive) was getting calls."[11] The grievances were heard by a Commissioner by the name of Reed. He ruled in favor of the workers.

Suddenly so much was happening. The Agricultural Workers Organizing Committee had opened an office nearby in Lindsay with Violet Rotan, "a born organizer," in charge. The NFWA's magazine, *El Malcriado*, was showing up in the barrios. The Church was getting involved having its little FWO organizing office in Porterville. And ordained ministers were mixed up in it.

In the Spring of 1965, the Tulare County Community Development staff encouraged the leaders of the Farm Workers Organization to consider affiliation with the NFWA. In a split vote, the FWO chose in April 1965 to affiliate with Chavez's organization. "It was the only way we could see to tie this group of farm workers to the issue they cared about most—protection from exploitation on the job."[12]

EMPOWERMENT BUILDS COURAGE

Some of the people who filed grievances on their sugar beet wages lived in the Woodville and Linnell farm labor camps. They were under the jurisdiction of the Tulare County Housing Authority. In 1965 the Housing Authority condemned these tin shacks. Then they raised the rents from $18 to $22 a month as a way to get money to improve them.

Residents of the camp were angry that the rents were being raised on these miserable old shacks that Eleanor Roosevelt had dedicated in the '30's. The Champion family, veterans of the sugar beet case, organized a rent strike at the Woodville camp, which was between Porterville and Tipton. It spread to the Linnell camp. Residents began paying rent into a trust fund.

As the rent strike gathered momentum, a big march was planned for July 16, 1965 from the Linnell camp to the County Court House—five miles. Drake organized some outside people to march with the farm workers. I was among those recruited. We got a tour of the Linnell camp. The one room metal shacks had 15 amp wiring, outside spigots for water, a community bathroom in terrible condition, all set on a big dirt lot. It was a run-down dump.

After the tour, we were paired up and wound out of the camp in a long line. In the lead, wearing his clerical collar, was a tall, slender young man named Brother Gilbert. He was vice-principal of Garces High School in Bakersfield. His high visibility was both useful and a shocker. This was in the diocese of Bishop Willinger, an 87 year old priest who "was personal friends of all the major growers in the diocese, and just was no friend of the farm workers at all." [13] By Fall, 1965, Brother Gilbert, now known as LeRoy Chatfield, left the Christian Brothers and joined the staff of the NFWA.

THE NFWA STRIKES IN THE ROSES

In May of 1965, the NFWA decided to back the wage demands of rose cutters at the Mt. Arbor Nursery just south of Delano. The company had refused to bargain, and 60 of the 65 workers went on strike under the leadership of Chavez's NFWA. The CMM, "with some noticeable administrative nervousness," assigned Gilbert Padilla and Jim Drake to work on the strike. [14]

The CMM decided to use Jim Drake's case to work out policy concerning staff doing labor organizing. Drake intended to help the NFWA on the strike regardless of the policy decision. So the plan was to ask the CMM Commission and the UCC Conference Church and Community Commission to support Drake's participation in the NFWA strike. If they would not give their support, Drake would make it his vacation time. Both the CMM and UCC Commissions voted their support. "By that little action we found ourselves in the workers' movement," recalled the UCC's Dr. Norberg. He went on to comment that, "Sometimes big doors swing on little hinges." [15]

When the Commissions made their decisions to support Drake's participation in the NFWA strike it was on the grounds that it was consistent with his assigned task, "to help farm workers organize for self-help action of a kind that they define, targeted on goals they determine." Hartmire comments, "The CMM commitment to farm worker organizing was so strong by this time that no matter what the administrators decided, the field staff would have helped with the rose strike."[16] [17]

CESAR CHAVEZ

No explanation of the developing ties between the CMM and the NFWA can make sense without some understanding of who Cesar Chavez was, and is. The man is deeply religious, a gifted organizer, and fiercely committed to improving life for farm workers. The following section from Hartmire's 1967 paper provides some background on Chavez, and, at the same time, reflects Hartmire's regard for Chavez:

Cesar Chavez is an extraordinary leader and an accurate analysis of this struggle dare not underestimate the quality of that leadership. In 1951, Cesar was discovered in a San Jose barrio by Fred Ross, who at the time was building a militant grass-roots Mexican-American organization under the sponsorship of the Industrial Areas Foundation (IAF). The organization was called the Community Service Organization (CSO) . . . Eventually, Cesar Chavez became the national director of CSO . . .

In April of 1962, convinced that farm labor organizing was the primary need of the Mexican-American people and also convinced that CSO could not or would not take on that task, Chavez left his paid position with CSO and moved with his wife, Helen, and their eight children to Delano, California. Helen had been raised in Delano and she and Cesar had met there in the days when his family were migrant farm laborers . . . His purpose in the spring of 1962 was to begin to build a militant and democratic farm workers union that would be composed of farm workers, paid for by farm workers and run by farm workers. He traveled to every farming community in the San Joaquin Valley seeking out those farm workers who understood the need for organization and who would be willing to pay $3.50 dues monthly . . . During this initial period of building the NFWA, he had no salary.

He and his family worked in the fields when they were able. He accepted a small amount of financial support from a few selected people.

. . . On September 30, 1962 there was a founding convention of the NFWA in Fresno. Jim Drake and I were both present. By late 1963, Cesar was getting a salary of $40 per week. In September 1965, the NFWA had 2,000 family members, a service office in Delano, a credit union, death benefit insurance and additional staff.

. . . Cesar Chavez brought to the strike fourteen years of solid organizational experience and a deep commitment to serve farm workers.[18]

Chavez was raised a Roman Catholic in a rural area of Arizona. The family farm and store (later lost in the Depression) was a long way from town and a church. But he and his brothers and sisters were taught their faith at home. And he learned in his family that religious faith applies to all of life and must be demonstrated in the way you live, in the way you treat people.

Around the time Chavez began learning organizing from Fred Ross, a priest named Donald McDonnell was assigned to the San Jose barrio called Sal Si Puedes to gather a congregation. Chavez helped him in a variety of ways, and McDonnell introduced him to the Papal encyclicals, agribusiness economics, St. Francis, and Gandhi. Chavez was developing an idea of how to make change for farm workers, how to redress the suffering and humiliations that he and his family, and thousands of other families, had experienced as Mexican-Americans and as farm workers.

Chavez became a student of Gandhi. Gandhi's philosophy and nonviolent organizing techniques were formative in Chavez's development as an organizer and a nonviolent leader.

Chavez's commitment to nonviolence made possible the broad Church support that later developed for the farm labor struggle that was frequently marked by violent opposition from police, growers, Teamsters, and others.

The religious grounding of Chavez and of many of the workers provided a dependable place for thousands of middle class Christians to stand next to farm workers. A labor struggle was unfamiliar ground for the majority of middle class Christians. Most mainline Protestant denominations have had little, if any, contact with the American labor movement, had little involvement with Mexican-American communities, and tended to have only a missionary interest in Filipinos.

NFWA VOTES TO JOIN THE GRAPE STRIKE

The Agricultural Workers Organizing Committee (AWOC) of the AFL-CIO was stirring the pot in California under the leadership of Norman Smith, Al Green and the late Larry Itliong. They had struck for higher wages when the grapes were ready for harvest in the southern part of California in 1965. As the workers followed the harvest north, the ferment for better wages went with them. By September, the workers arrived in the Delano area vineyards. AWOC's members in Delano were mostly Filipinos, men with a long history of farm labor organizing. On September 8 they voted to strike in the Delano grapes. Members of the NFWA didn't want to cross AWOC's picket lines. So one week later, September 16, the NFWA voted to join AWOC on strike.

The NFWA did not feel prepared for a major strike. They didn't have the resources to support their people. But the decision was made and they would simply have to get what help they could.

Chavez, like Doug Still, had seen that the one institution with an interest in farm workers was the Church. He had no illusions about the willingness, at that time, of the Roman Catholic Church to threaten its ties with the agricultural establishment in order to help farm workers. But there was this little Protestant ministry, the CMM, that would help. Chavez had cultivated them, and they had cultivated their ties with Chavez. Now he would see how serious the CMM was.

Chavez later said, "(The CMM) were the first to come to our aid, financially and in every other way, and they spread the word to other benefactors."[19] Hartmire goes on to comment that, "As a matter of historical fact, the churches were the single most important source of support in the first ninety days of the Huelga (strike)."[20]

Jim Drake was immediately assigned to work with Chavez and the NFWA. He was the CMM's "inside man," able to keep the director informed of what was happening, what was needed, and what assignments the NFWA would like the Church to take.

Hartmire, recalling that time, said, "By the time the strike came in '65 it was probably humanly impossible for us to tell Cesar we couldn't help . . . Actually, Jim and I were planning to break with the Councils of Churches if we had to and form our own organization. But it never came to that . . . The field staff were too far into the farm worker community and clear about what it would take to bring about some humanizing of the situation. They wouldn't have stood for it if we had said, 'Sorry, this is too tough, too controversial.' "[21]

By 1965 there had already been eight years in which Fred Ross, Cesar Chavez, and others gave organizing training to CMM staff. Cesar Chavez and his wife, Helen, and their children had been coming regularly to CMM bimonthly staff retreats. The CMM staff believed deeply in Chavez and "his grassroots approach to farm labor organizing." They understood community organizing to be a form of servant ministry consistent with Jesus' life and work. Hartmire wrote:

Most of the necessary preparation took place because of a basic decision on the part of the CMM to go with the people and be their servants to the limit of our ability to understand and to serve. This decision which was made and re-made by a number of people at the staff and policy level over a period of nearly a decade led the CMM into deep fellowship with farm workers and their key leaders . . . Without this pioneering penetration, the church would not have been in a position to understand the strikers or support them in their time of need; nor would we have been able to bring our influence and our hopefulness about life to bear in a tense and at times hopeless situation. Gospel communication and influence are tied inextricably to servanthood. There does not seem to be any other way!"[22]

THE NONVIOLENT ACTION PROGRAM

By the time 1965 rolled around and the grape strike had begun in Delano, it was not easy to get support in the churches, especially the San Joaquin Valley churches, which had been the mainstay of CMM support over the years. There was nervousness and some opposition in the churches to community organizing. Direct support for a union on strike was really tough to sell. Valley church people were thinking about the economic threat of workers getting organized. And to many, a strike seemed like a violent, confrontive, unchristian endeavor.

But Cesar Chavez and Chris Hartmire convinced a lot of church people in the agricultural areas, and even more in the cities, that this was a nonviolent movement and the churches ought to support it. Chavez accomplished this through his genius as an organizer and strategist. Hartmire's contribution was as a superb and indefatigable communicator and leader.

Many people think of a nonviolent group as simply one that does not use violence. But in a social change movement the simple absence of violence could never be sustained without an action program. People who get involved in a change movement are angry. Justice has been denied. They want change and they want to see results.

U.S. farm workers are no more prone to pacifism than other people in the United States. They agreed to try a nonviolent approach because Chavez asked them to, and they respected him. If his approach had had no success, I seriously doubt that the movement would have continued without violence on the part of the strikers.

Now here's the point. The nonviolent stance of the movement attracted a lot of moral support. The action program gave form for the moral support—gave people something to do. And the actual working participation of so many people was a critical factor in keeping the movement nonviolent.

Cesar Chavez says in *Autobiography of la Causa*, "The whole essence of nonviolent action is getting a lot of people involved, vast numbers doing little things." But have you ever contemplated starting a movement involving thousands of people? I can have an anxiety attack just thinking about it. It's an enormous responsibility. The farm worker leadership has had the guts to take responsibility for a nonviolent program, which from the very beginning involved over a thousand farm workers, and at the peak of the table grape boycott included 17 million U.S. citizens who refused to buy grapes. It even attracted international support from union members who would not handle the grapes.

The farm worker leadership has not come to the Church simply describing what a terrible life farm workers have, how sad and unjust it is. They have come saying, "There has been injustice and we intend to correct it. We need your help, and this is what you can do. We need food and money for our strikers. We need the presence of clergy and lay religious on our picket lines. We need your support for our economic boycotts." Their requests have been absolutely clear and definitely within the scope of what church people *can* do.

Not everyone welcomed Chavez's decision that the movement be nonviolent. There were people involved in the Delano strike who disagreed. And there were people in the wider labor movement who thought it was a mistake. When Cesar insisted on nonviolence he lost some support, according to Jerry Cohen, who was General Counsel for the Union. He lost that support in a gamble that he could get and hold support from the churches. Support from the churches was an essential ingredient in keeping the movement nonviolent; giving encouragement to the strikers (strike lines can be very boring, tedious, isolating, and sometimes frightening); assuring that the national news media would send reporters and photographers several hundred miles to cover the strike.

Having said that, it is necessary to say that the importance of the Church would have been nil if there had not been a vibrant, well-led Union for the Church to help.

The next two chapters describe the nonviolent action program of the United Farm Workers (see Appendix for name changes that occur), and how it engaged people of faith and the institutions of the Church. Chapter 2 has the stories of church people from the cities who traveled to be with farm workers in the fields. Chapter 3 has stories from the boycotts and how the farm workers brought the struggle to the towns and cities of the continent, and the surprising responses of the Church and church people to the opportunities to boycott wines, grapes, lettuce, supermarkets, drug stores, liquor chains, Purex Bleach, and the Dow Chemical Company.

CHAPTER 2

Meeting Farm Workers In the Fields

> *It was the first time on an issue I had physically moved my body to a different place. It did a different thing in a sense of investment . . . To move your body and be in their setting rather than your own, to see faces and hear voices. There is a different sense of the passion of the issue. It was less possible to distance from it.*
>
> Dr. James Stewart

IN WHAT WAYS DID Church supporters enter into the farm workers' movement at the primary sites—in the agricultural valleys of California and Arizona? What happened to Church supporters as a result of their participation "in the fields?" To answer these questions, we'll examine five historic periods lifted out of constant involvement during the decade 1965–1975.

ON THE STRIKELINES IN DELANO

The strike had begun on September 8, 1965. Soon the most serious problem for the strikers was police harassment. Police ignored violence against the strikers, while "violence by the strikers was aggressively investigated and punished."¹ The Kern County sheriff admitted he was keeping a file on everyone who walked on a picket line. No such file was kept on employers and their personnel. By early October, Kern County Sheriff's deputies told picketers they could not talk to workers in the fields. "The roving picket lines were trying to cover 400 square miles of grape vineyards and in order to persuade workers to join the strike they had to be able to talk with them."² They were specifically banned from shouting "huelga" (Spanish for strike).

Under these circumstances, identifiable clergy and religious supporters on the picket lines were useful for several reasons: to remind local police that people from outside the area were watching this action; to back-up the nonviolent stance of the strikers; to further involve the Church in the strike. At first the only religious support was Migrant Ministry staff walking picket lines with the workers. On October 17, 1965, a striker was told by police that he could not read Jack London's definition of a strikebreaker to people in the fields. The Rev. David Havens, of the CMM, "read the piece in place of the worker and was immediately arrested."³

On October 19, 1965, six weeks into the strike, a group of Church supporters from outside the area joined the strikers to test the ban on shouting "huelga" on the picket line. They were there at the request of the Migrant Ministry for a "Demonstration of Christian Concern". One of the clergymen, Charles McLain, recalls that day.

Cecil (Hoffman) had asked me to go to Delano to be on a strike line. So I went. There was a group of 50 or so clergy, including Bob Brown. We met with Cesar in the social hall of the Seventh Day Adventist Church for a briefing. Cesar had heard that the police would be arresting strikers for disturbing the peace. Cesar informed the group of that possibility and was very gracious in letting them decide whether they found it workable to risk being arrested at that time. Some decided to leave after the afternoon training and dinner at Filipino Hall. But a group of us stayed and spent the night.

The next morning we were assigned a ranch to go to. When we arrived at the entrance where our group was to picket, sheriff's deputies were already there. I heard one radioing to ranch personnel, 'Don't send workers here. A group of clergy are here.' The scales fell from my eyes. I just kept saying, 'The police are helping the growers.' Others in my group thought me naive to be surprised at that.

Later that day when we had all joined a picket line, we were arrested. Even Chris Hartmire who was supposed to be our outside contact person if we were arrested. He was dragged out of his car and thrown in the police van. Forty-four of us were arrested.

The news media were there that day and a photograph of our group appeared in TIME magazine. We were also seen on television. I was the only clergy in the group serving a local church. People in my congregation were very upset. One man in the church had a brother who was a grape grower in Delano.''[4]

Of the forty-four arrested thirty-four were strikers (Chavez's wife, Helen, among them), nine clergy, and a lay supporter. The next year the Kern County District Attorney dropped the charges against the forty-four.[5] Also a Bakersfield judge dismissed the charges against Havens on the grounds that he had the constitutional right to stand on public property and read from Jack London. "From that time on, the picket line had the freedom it needed."[6]

The presence of clergy and lay leaders from outside the area on the picket lines focused attacks by growers and local ministers on the Migrant Ministry. Mark Day notes some of the reactions in his book *Forty Acres*. He recalls Delano grower Bruno Dispoto saying, "We are sincerely looking forward to the day when we get rid of outside agitators, rabble rousers, college kooks, migrant ministers and priests."[7]

Day also recalls the Delano Ministerial Association denouncing the actions of the visiting clergy and stating that it was not the function of churchmen to organize farm workers.[8]

But complaints and opposition did nothing to deter the Migrant Ministry from organizing one of the most operative national networks of support that the Church has seen on a social issue. What the opposition was seeing was only the beginning of waves of Church supporters and students, many organized by the Migrant Ministry as an assignment they took from the Union. The presence of outside supporters was one of the few safeguards for the strikers.

Chavez recalled some of the injustice and violence against the workers during the first two years of the strike. "Some of our pickets were sprayed with pesticides. Others had dogs turned on them, and guns discharged over their heads. We had cases where our cars were turned over, and one case where a grower drove into one of our pickets. And we were never able to get a complaint against him."[9]

SACRAMENTO MARCH

Chavez had long had an interest in the Mexican religious traditions of processions and pilgrimages. Later they took on meaning for others to whom the forms were new.

In early Spring 1966, anticipating Lent, Chavez and the workers decided to make a pilgrimage from Delano to Sacramento, the California State Capital. The external reasons for the march were to call attention to the strike, to take their case to the Governor, Edmund G. (Pat) Brown, Sr., and "to take the strike to the workers outside the Delano area, because they weren't too enthused. They were frightened, and they didn't really know what was happening."[10] The Union's first boycott, which was against Schenley products, had begun the previous December, though the boycott was not a feature of the March. It became a highlight during the last week, when Schenley became the first Delano grower to recognize the Union as a bargaining agent for the workers.

The internal, spiritual reasons for the pilgrimage gave the external objectives power. The theme of the March was "Peregrinacion, Penitencia, Revolucion", pilgrimage, penitence, and revolution. Editions of *El Malcriado* in Spanish and English and Tagalog (a Filipino language) spelled out the meaning of the March. *"Peregrinacion:* The pilgrimage stands not as a protest by Delano workers, but as a symbol of the needs of all the farm workers. *Penitencia:* The sufferings of the march are a penance for the sins of everyone—on both sides of this bitter fight. *Revolucion:* The march is a bid for the extension of the benefits of the great revolutions of America and of Mexico to the poor of California. It is not just a demand for higher wages; it is the cause of a whole people who have been robbed of their dignity."[11]

Jim Drake, CMM staff person and administrative assistant to Chavez, measured the distance to Sacramento and found it was about three hundred miles. Logistical arrangements for the March: cars to pick up people with sore feet, food for marchers, places to sleep, and fiestas at night, were organizing opportunities. There was so much people could do.

And there was walking. Sixty-seven strikers were selected to form the core of the pilgrimage, to walk the entire three hundred miles. But from the very first day others joined them. In fact, the strikers might not have been allowed to walk out of Delano except for the presence of clergy and supportive labor officials. The Delano police tried to block their route out of town.

The pilgrimage took place during Lent. And toward the end it was vacation time, and a season set apart for special observances. As the 67 *originales* made their way, step by step up the Valley, people joined them, first dozens, then hundreds and then thousands. On Easter Sunday 10,000 filed across the bridge and into Sacramento.

Catholic Doors Open

Jim Drake remembers the March: "The big turning point (for the Union) came when the march to Sacramento took place. I believe Bishop Willinger was retired, and I believe Bishop Manning came from Stockton, where he was something of a liberal up there. I believe that's when he came to Fresno. When we got to Fresno the doors of the Catholic churches began to open up to us.''

But why did the doors open up? It was certainly not just because a more liberal Bishop had arrived in the Fresno Diocese. The people themselves, working people, poor people, farm workers, up and down the Valley recognized the symbols of the March, felt connected to what they saw and understood of this pilgrimage.

Drake recalled the debate that took place the night before the March was to begin over whether the Virgin of Guadalupe, patron saint of Mexico, would lead the March. The question was "whether or not you could mix religious symbolism with a working class movement." It was decided that the Virgin would lead the March. The decision "leveraged open all kinds of Catholic doors through the Valley. I never knew if they were doing it for the Virgin or for the marchers, but they would put all this food out when we would march into a town. The theme . . . took on a very religious meaning. Whether the priest liked it or not, the working class people of the church were there with the doors open.''

A basic organizing precept of Saul Alinsky's was always to operate within the experience of your people and outside the experience of your opponents. Drake felt the strategy of the pilgrimage to Sacramento was a classic example of this precept. "The opponents never could understand. It confounded the Marxists to the left and the farmers to the right. They never could figure out what the Virgin had to do with this whole thing. The people saw the movement in keeping with Mexican revolutionary experience, and it was led by someone with deep respect for the ancestors. And some believed that the Virgin guaranteed success.''[12] With or without the support of pastors the doors of Catholic churches flew open in towns all along the line of march, and many farm workers in these parishes joined the marchers.

Other people started paying attention to the "Huelga" too, because of publicity for the March, and because it was an opportunity to participate. Among these were Dr. Richard Norberg, of the United Church of Christ, and Fr. Eugene Boyle, a priest in the San Francisco Diocese, Loris Coletta, president at that time of United Church Women for Southern California and Nevada, and myself, my husband and our nine year old son, and many others. Following are some recollections of the meaning of the March to supporters.

Dr. Richard Norberg, who was Conference Minister for the Northern California Conference of the United Church of Christ in 1966, joined the March just outside Sacramento. What especially has stuck in his memory is the integrity of the religious experience of Easter morning worship outside of Sacramento.

I remember when Cesar was leading his walk from down in the Valley to Sacramento. I was due to attend (the Easter service) in a church in Stockton or Lodi, I don't recall. But I went up on Saturday and walked the last portion with them to a school house building. Someone had gotten some flowers and put them in a milk bottle on a stand, and there was a worship experience in that building, devoid of all the lilies, but with the fervor of that walk and what it meant. I entered fully into that and felt so good. We were there expressing thanks to God on Easter morning. I'll never forget my feeling when I had to leave. There was a terrible tug of emotion for me.[13]

Father Eugene Boyle was a priest in the San Francisco Diocese and was chair of their Commission on Social Justice. The Commission had received a call for people to join the March, and he responded. The first time he saw Chavez was on the March. "He was on a cane the first time I saw him, and he would occasionally rest in the back of a station wagon that was traveling along with the March."

Fr. Boyle had joined the March at two or three different points and soon was organizing others to participate. "I joined the

March (again) on Holy Saturday outside the State Capital and marched with them to the Capitol (on Easter Sunday) and spoke there. What I had tried to do, along with Bill Kircher (of the AFL-CIO), was to induce Governor Pat Brown to be there. We called him on the phone down at Frank Sinatra's place in Palm Springs . . . He refused to come up. But Bill and I worked on it the night before, both of us phoning. From that time I began to really get involved."[14]

Another person who joined the March for the final weekend was Loris Coletta, of United Church Women for Southern California and Nevada. UCW had been a leader in work with migrants for years, but support of the strike was another thing. Loris herself had never been involved in anything of this kind. Her family was shocked by her participation in the March and many of the parishioners in the wealthy congregation, of which her husband was the pastor, could not understand her involvement. But she had met Chavez during 1965 and she trusted him as a religious man and a nonviolent leader.

"The Sacramento march was a highlight for me. We stopped by a river. I saw these three young men who were carrying three crosses . . . I remember coming back to my church and trying to explain that not only was this a movement for justice but it was a spiritual movement. I noticed the looks of horror on the faces of people in my congregation."[15]

My husband, Cecil, our nine year old son, Bruce, and I drove from Los Angeles to Sacramento to walk the last few miles of the March. Though I had been helping in a variety of ways in Los Angeles, this was my first participation in an event in the Valley. I generally stayed close to home with our three children, the youngest of them only a toddler. It was an opportunity for me to return to the agricultural valley where we had lived for three years, from 1958 to 1961, and where I had first become acquainted with the situation of farm workers.

When last I had been with farm workers in 1961 they were dispirited, hat in hand, disorganized, with little to hope for. When I joined the March I saw a great change. The farm workers were organized and determined. They were walking with Church leaders from many denominations, national labor leaders and rank and file proudly carrying banners identifying their unions and locals, and Congressmen. The week before they reached Sacramento, word came that Schenley Liquors had agreed to negotiate. It was the first break in the seven month old Delano strike.

On Easter Sunday, we marched through the streets of Sacramento to the Capitol steps where a rally was planned. As the procession began arriving at the rally site, visiting dignitaries filled up the few chairs. But a member of the Union went to the microphone and asked that the chairs be vacated—they were for the 67 farm workers who had walked all the way from Delano. The order of things was changing.

A DIFFICULT TIME

During the period from the Sacramento March in Spring of 1966 to early Spring of 1968, the Union had taken on the large corporate grape growers in the Delano area. These were not small town farmers. Many had their corporate offices in high rise buildings in San Francisco and Los Angeles, with national and international marketing divisions and company attorneys. Between March 1966 and March 1968, the Union had organized at the giant DiGiorgio Corporation ranches. The UFW took on and won recognition from six large wineries: Perelli-Minetti, Almaden, Christian Brothers, Gallo, Paul Masson, and Franzia. The Teamsters kept cropping up in sweetheart deals with growers who were under pressure to sign contracts with the UFW. So during this two year period there were multiple strikes, boycotts, elections, arbitrations, contract negotiations, and working to keep the Union itself staffed, funded, and functioning. (It was during this period that the two organizations which had worked together on the strike, the Agricultual Workers Organizing Committee (AWOC) of the AFL-CIO, and Chavez' National Farm Workers Association (NFWA) merged becoming the United Farm Workers Organizing Committee, AFL-CIO (UFWOC). For simplicity I will refer to it as the UFW.)

In August of 1967, the workers at the Giumarra Vineyards voted to go out on strike. Giumarra was the largest table grape grower in the world. This was the beginning of a difficult and often discouraging struggle.

Father Mark Day came to Delano after the Giumarra strike began. In his book, *Forty Acres*, he recalls the strike and the sacrifices the workers made. He recounts the workers' daily schedule of rising at 4:30 a.m. in order to be with a group on a picket line before dawn. He says, "By this time, the strikebreakers had become what the strikers called 'hard-core scabs.' They looked upon the strikers with contempt, thumbed their noses at the pickets, and made obscene gestures at the women strikers." At 8 a.m. the strikers would return home to get the children off to school. Then they would report to the union offices to work until early evening.

Fr. Day himself became "discouraged and depressed at the lack of progress and the seeming hopelessness of the situation." He goes on to say, "In the early Spring of 1968, Cesar feared that violence was an imminent danger. Pickets were harassed daily. The strikers had become jumpy and were beginning to feel defeated."[16]

The Union was boycotting Giumarra's grapes across the nation. Boycotting table grapes was much more difficult than boycotting something that came with a label attached to the product, like a bottle of Gallo wine. But diligent supporters around the country, urged on by boycott staff, were going into stores demanding to see the boxes the grapes came in and picketing the stores that carried Giumarra grapes. This strategy was reasonably effective until Giumarra was found to be using the labels of other growers. It was this tactic that led to the now famous Grape Boycott, a boycott of all table grapes.

I hope the reader can use imagination to picture this two year period culminating in a difficult strike and boycott. Through this whole period, with thousands of strikers and many incidents of violence and taunting, the Union had been able to keep the movement nonviolent. But the workers were becoming more discouraged. Chavez had had to confiscate a few guns on the picket line.[17] What should a leader do in such a situation?

Chavez decided to fast.

CHAVEZ'S 25 DAY FAST

On February 14, 1968 Chavez announced to the membership that he had begun a personal, religious fast. He spent the water-only fast period, which lasted 25 days, at Forty Acres, the Union's headquarters in Delano. He stayed in a small room in the adobe gas station the members had built.

How could fasting make a difference? Levy remembers Chavez saying he felt it was necessary "to bring the Movement to a halt, to do something that would force them and me to deal with the whole question of violence and ourselves."[18] Chavez recalled what he told the workers when he announced his fast. "I told them I thought they were discouraged, because they were talking about short cuts, about violence. They were getting so mad with the growers, that they couldn't be effective anymore . . . Then I said I was going to stop eating until such time as everyone in the strike either ignored me or made up their minds that they were not going to be committing violence."[19]

The personal pain and sacrifice of Chavez's fast quickly became the focus of the strike and the boycott. Mark Day recalls, "We offered Mass each night at the adobe gas station . . . Nationwide

TV audiences caught the prayer, penance, and nonviolence themes of the fast. I am sure Cesar got his point across, and I am convinced that much of our present support was generated during that period."[20]

Chavez's sacrifice inspired others to sacrifice as well. Members and supporters began working harder. Many people on the boycott fasted. Organizer Marshall Ganz fasted for ten days. Chavez's brother, Richard, fasted. Dolores Huerta, a leader in the Union, fasted. According to Dolores, "By that fast he was able to unify the farm workers all over the state of California. Prior to that fast, there had been a lot of bickering and backbiting and fighting and little attempts at violence. But Cesar brought everybody together and really established himself as the leader of the farm workers."[21]

But not everyone in the Union was inspired by the Fast. According to Jerry Cohen, "A lot of people didn't like it. People left the Union over that. So it was a committment to a certain kind of religious involvement that offended a lot of fairly ideological left types. It was an internal crisis." Cohen said the Fast was a watershed for what support Chavez would get, losing ideologues from the Left and consolidating religious support.

The Fast ended on March 11, 1968 with a Mass and celebration at Delano's Memorial Park. A throng of thousands was there to be part of this important event. The Fast had begun as Chavez's private spiritual act. It had become public and had involved thousands who, because of Chavez's act, had deepened their own committment to nonviolent change for farm workers.

I was in the throng that day. My family and I had moved from Los Angeles to Colton, California, a town about 60 miles east of Los Angeles. I found two women friends who were interested in going with me to Delano. Neither of them had had direct contact with the Union before. Both were active in the Presbyterian Church in Colton. None of us was accustomed to traveling without our husbands. One of the women had a good car, but was afraid to drive the long distance to Delano. I was afraid also, but didn't admit it. So I drove her car and the three of us were able to take part in the event.

Mark Day recalls the scene in *Forty Acres*:

Cesar, who had lost thirty-five pounds, sat weak and immobile next to Helen, and his mother, and the late Senator Robert Kennedy . . . the Mass was ecumenical in nature. Jerome Lackner, Cesar's personal physician, read the first passage, from the Old Testament. Lackner is Jewish. A Protestant minister took the second reading, and a Catholic priest, the third . . .

Following the Mass, we distributed over three hundred loaves of Mexican semita bread. We blessed the bread and called it the bread of social justice . . . The Reverend Jim Drake, Cesar's administrative assistant and a member of the California Migrant Ministry, read a statement for Chavez. . . . Kennedy spoke amid the cheers of the workers . . . Paul Schrade, West Coast director for the United Auto Workers and a close friend of Cesar's, presented to the union a check for $50,000, on behalf of Walter Reuther.[22]

Jim Drake recently talked about the Fast and the people who called it manipulation of religious symbols. But Drake said the Fast showed "a guy who was willing to put his life on the line, and make that investment, which has to be more than just strategic or tactical. It was much more fundamental, a matter of commitment." Drake felt that the Fast was a turning point for Chavez and in some ways limited him. "After that he was a guru instead of a general . . . After that he could not make mistakes," according to Drake. People's expectations for Chavez had become extraordinary.

THE BISHOPS' COMMITTEE

In late 1969, the UFW was going full blast on the grape boycott, trying to get a breakthrough with table grape growers. In four years of strikes and boycotts, the only contracts were with wineries. The table grape boycott, undertaken because growers were letting Giumarra use their labels, was against 850 growers in California and Arizona, an enormous job.

The UFW contacted the National Conference of Catholic Bishops (NCCB) asking for their endorsement of the boycott. The NCCB had never endorsed a boycott. "They weren't that kind of organization," according to Monsignor George Higgins, who was a labor specialist with the Conference. But Higgins prepared a boycott endorsement and the Conference considered it. Some of the California Bishops wanted to find another way to support the right of the farm workers to bargain collectively. They decided to withhold endorsement of the boycott but form a committee to mediate the impasse between the growers and the UFW.

The Bishops' prestige was clearly a factor in finally getting the growers to talk with the UFW. Many of the growers wanted to settle but didn't want to be the first. The international boycott was hurting them. In July table grape growers had filed a seventy-five million dollar suit against the UFW claiming "the boycott has caused losses of twenty-five million dollars to grape growers."[23] A committee of Bishops coming to them personally and asking them to meet provided the breakthrough needed. Negotiating sessions began in Coachella and moved in stages up the Valleys. It was the first time the Delano growers had ever talked with Chavez.

Mark Day comments in his book on the uniqueness of the Bishops' action. "It was the first time in the history of the Church in the United States that the Roman Catholic hierarchy had taken such a direct role in a major labor dispute . . . Its effectiveness was and is proof that the institutional church can make meaningful contributions to contemporary social problems."[24]

The Bishops' Committee's mediation, while special, is only one of many examples of ways individuals and institutions of the Church entered into the farm workers' struggle in significant ways, using the skills, expertise, and openings available to them. Every such act on behalf of justice is a credit to the actors. I want to underline that such acts would have had no stage if the UFW had not set one. The Church would have had no cue line if the UFW had not taken responsibility for an over-all strategy. And there would have been little impact if innumerable farm workers had not risen at 4:30 a.m. to go out on strike lines, and traveled to distant cities on the boycott to tell their stories to strangers. Their vision, their sacrifices made the Church's contributions possible and efficacious.

Rev. Lloyd Saatjian, a United Methodist pastor in Palm Springs, was another important figure in mediating the first contracts, which were with growers in the Coachella Valley near Palm Springs. The first contract was signed in April 1970 in the Chancery office of the Los Angeles Archdiocese.

The work of the Bishops' Committee did not end with the signing of contracts in 1970. It continued to play a critical role as the focus of the struggle moved to the vegetable growing area of the coastal Salinas Valley. In particular, Bishop Donnelly, chairman of the Committee with twenty-five years of experience in labor mediation, and Monsignor Higgins, staff to the Committee, played crucial and long-suffering roles in arbitrating the grower/Teamster collusion against the UFW.

SUMMER OF 1973

I've picked out several events or periods of supporter involvement with the UFW in the agricultural areas from a decade of heavy, continuous organizing. But for sheer numbers of supporters and intensity there was no time like the Summer of 1973. All the grape contracts, so painfully won in 1970, were expiring in 1973. The growers' strategy was to sign sweetheart contracts with the Teamsters to keep the UFW out. This would give the growers the appearance of unionization without power changing hands. The growers could return to nearly total control, ending this brief time of power sharing with their workers. No more worker control over pesticide use, no more necessity to hire through the union hiring hall with its fairness rules to protect older employees, no more listening to grievances brought by formerly docile field hands.

Teamster leadership had no real interest in organizing farm labor. (Many in the rank and file of the Teamsters had an entirely different attitude than the leadership.) Einar Mohn, of the Western Conference of Teamsters was reported in the *Los Angeles Times* on April 28, 1973 as saying that farm workers would not be able to take part in Teamster Union meetings "for about two years" when he expected more whites and fewer Mexicans in California agriculture.

The growers' obstinance, and the Teamsters' racism was capped by their unprecedented violence. The UFW was literally fighting for its life that summer. When contracts were not renewed, the workers struck in one area after another as the harvest moved from the Coachella Valley in the South up to the central San Joaquin Valley. The picket lines were countered by armed growers and Teamster hired goons. The *Los Angeles Times* reported 350 Teamster hired "guards" in the Coachella Valley.[25]

The UFW worked frantically organizing the strike, keeping it nonviolent, trying to feed and support hundreds and hundreds of strikers and their families. The Migrant Ministry not only raised a lot of money for food but gave a large amount from its own budget to feed farm workers. And the Ministry took the assignment to keep religious supporters on the picket lines to protect the strikers and to keep both sides as cool as possible.

Many dramatic stories came out of that summer from ordinary middle class supporters who agreed to enter into the frightening and sometimes violent encounters on the strike lines. I will relate two of those stories, one of Protestant supporters in the Coachella Valley, and the other centering around Catholic support when the harvest reached the Fresno area.

THE UNITED CHURCH OF CHRIST RESPONDS

At the beginning of the book I told part of the story of the United Church of Christ delegation that took a charter flight from their General Synod meeting in St. Louis, Missouri, to California's Coachella Valley in June of 1973.

There were big issues to discuss at the Synod meeting, among them the continuing upheaval in Cambodia and the Watergate scandal. John Moyer, on the staff of the UCC Board of Homeland Ministries, and their representative on the Board of the NFWM, had prepared a resolution supporting both the grape and lettuce boycotts. His plan was to try to pass this resolution. Then came the call from Chavez saying the Teamsters had "unleashed a campaign of violence against farm workers on strike in Coachella and Arvin" in California and asking if a small delegation from the meeting could come to Coachella to encourage nonviolence.

Things had gotten very rough in Coachella. The Campos family, who were strikers, barely escaped from their trailer when it was burned down. Strikers had had their car windows shot out or stoned.[26]

There was an extraordinary ground swell of support at the Synod meeting for the UFW and for nonviolence. One person wanted to charter two 747's and send the entire General Synod to Coachella. John Moyer could picture the UFW and Chris Hartmire going crazy making arrangements for that many people. Moyer phoned Hartmire and asked, "Can you handle one plane load?" The answer was yes. The next steps were decisions on who would get to go, arrangements for an airplane, and figuring who would pay for the plane. The whole well-planned Synod meeting was disrupted. Moyer recalled that the denomination had paid process consultants $35,000 to plan the meeting. "And we had totally overturned the process. We had completely upset the whole apple cart."

The meeting had begun on Friday. By Sunday evening all arrangements had been made and the Synod commissioned ninety-five people (nearly a fourth of the delegates) to go on behalf of the whole body to the Coachella Valley. John Moyer, of course, went with the group. They carried with them the flag of the United Church of Christ. They left St. Louis at 9:30 p.m. and arrived at the Ontario Airport in Southern California at 1:30 a.m. where they waited until 3:30 for three Greyhound busses to take them to the Coachella Valley.

Moyer rode in the lead bus. He had already been out to Coachella and knew what to expect. He directed the bus driver to go by the Safeway grocery store in town. "The Safeway parking lot had one very bright mercury vapor lamp. This was where the thugs hired by the Teamsters would meet about 3:30 or 4:00 in the morning to pick up their various baseball bats and chains and stuff that they were taking to the picket line that day . . . And as we came to it there they all were. People asked, 'Who are they?' 'Those are the people you are going to meet on the picket line today,'" Moyer replied.

From there they went to the Coachella Park, "literally into the arms of about 500 farm workers. It was a very moving thing. Cesar had driven all night from Bakersfield to be there when the busses came in."

Chris Hartmire recounted that many of the UCC delegates came as objective observers with an assignment to report back on their observations. But the strikers were scared and worried because the strikers' trailer had been burned down and there were rumors, later proved unfounded, of the death of a picket captain. So when the busses arrived carrying nearly one hundred support people from the Church the strikers gratefully, exultantly surrounded the busses clapping and cheering and embracing them. The UCC people were taken onto the small stage at the park and introduced one by one to the cheering, clapping, singing crowd. "By picket line time there was no space in that park for 'objectivity'", said Hartmire.

They were divided into groups of eight, and they were taken out to various picket lines. "St. Louis that year was very hot, temperatures were in the mid to upper nineties and very muggy. When we got to Coachella it was already that warm at 4:30 in the morning, and it got up to about 115 degrees at noontime."

During that day the supporters witnessed violence on the picket line. About two hundred Teamsters charged one picket line with rubber hoses, clubs, ice picks and guns. Five strikers required hospitalization and many more were injured. Though not any of the UCC delegation was injured, they witnessed some of the violence. Some "confronted violent people for the first time. We also saw the performance of one of the best police forces I've ever known, the Riverside County Sheriff's deputies . . . You could not see a more opposite police force than that one and the one in Kern County. The difference between night and day."[27]

They flew back 24 hours after they had left. The delegates, having had almost no sleep since well before they left St. Louis, were welcomed back with shouts of "Viva la huelga." It sounded like a UFW rally when they entered the hall. In plenary session all ninety-five filed before the microphone and each gave testimony about the meaning of the pilgrimage. Ann Cohen, the official spokesperson for the group, said, "Let us make the farm worker story our story, and pledge ourselves to struggle and share with them until we all have won. It is time for human liberation."[28]

Those who had stayed behind had their own experience. Dr. Richard Norberg, Northern California Conference Minister, suggested that as an expression of support for the Pilgrims that those who remained present a witness at a local market carrying California grapes there in St. Louis.[29]

People were deeply affected by their experiences, particularly the Pilgrims. "People who went on that plane became a network for five or six years after, who would support any action we would take among the churches. One of the people who went was a member of the Farm Bureau from Illinois. When he came back he was totally converted to the UFW's position. There is nothing like an event like that for education."[30]

When the grape harvest was over in the Coachella Valley, the action moved north into the San Joaquin Valley. The journey from south to north was lined with expiring contracts.

In Jacques Levy's book, Chavez recalls the events as the strike moved north with grower after grower refusing to renew UFW contracts and making deals with the Teamsters. Unlike in Riverside County, the county sheriffs of the four San Joaquin Valley counties were blatantly in the camp of the growers.

The UFW film, "Fighting For Our Lives," is a record of the violence of the sheriffs in the San Joaquin Valley that summer. It documents what Chavez called "a legal goon squad" in riot gear macing people, beating people with night sticks, making hundreds of illegal arrests in addition to thousands of arrests for breaking injunctions against picketing. There were 3,589 arrests that summer.[31]

Church supporters were in constant demand, both to witness what was going on and to limit the violence that the sheriffs' deputies felt free to unleash on poor people. My husband and I traveled to Arvin, in the Southern San Joaquin Valley, after we heard of mass arrests in Kern County. When we arrived at the gathering place, the city park in the early morning, it was crowded with women and teenage girls. Virtually all the men and boys were in jail. No arrests were made that day because the jails were full.

The largest number of arrests was in Fresno County where 1,993 people were jailed. Seventy of these were priests, nuns, and the well-known Catholic lay leader, Dorothy Day, who was 76 at the time of her arrest in Fresno.

That July there was a large, national symposium on Ignatian spirituality taking place in San Francisco. It drew many Jesuit priests as well as major superiors of men and women and delegates from other religious communities. Rose Cecilia Harrington, CSJ, attended that symposium. She recalls that the farm worker struggle had been referred to several times during the meeting. At the conclusion of the symposium everyone was asked to consider going to Fresno to be with the striking farm workers.

Sr. Rose Cecilia was one of many from the meeting who went to Parlier in Fresno County. They drove all night to be there at dawn for the daily meeting from which everyone was dispersed to different ranches for picketing. Chris Hartmire, of the Migrant Ministry, remembers addressing the religious supporters and giving them a choice of two different picket lines—one where there was an injunction and the other where there was no injunction. He informed them of how many workers were in jail including lots of non-working spouses with kids staying home with relatives. "We made clear that going to jail was the most helpful thing to do. Quite a few of the busy priests resented the moral dilemma we dropped on them at 5 A.M." Sr. Rose Cecilia remembers that Hartmire was asked how long they might be in jail. He said a day or two. "I remember being off by myself in the park, away from the three women I had come with. And I remember thinking that there wasn't any reason why I couldn't do this. So I went with a group of pickets to an orchard." The entire group was arrested and the women were taken to the Fresno County Industrial Farm. After being booked, Sr. Rose Cecilia, fifteen other nuns and a group of farm worker women were placed in a huge recreational room. They were held there for two nights. The nuns had been asked not to accept any special privileges not accorded the strikers, and not to be released on their own recognizance (O.R.) unless the strikers were also. As it turned out, none of the nuns was considered eligible for O.R. because they had full time jobs and were from other counties. The courts, therefore, considered them bad risks for showing up for trial.

After two days they were moved to a large dormitory. They got themselves organized for what turned out to be a two week stay in jail. Sr. Rose Cecilia remembers that Catherine Morris organized morning exercise. Another sister insisted that ordinary jail rules against men and women being together must be suspended because the inmates required daily mass. So two priests came from Fresno each day for Mass in the gymnasium. The women organized language lessons with the strikers teaching Spanish and the nuns teaching English to each other.[32]

The men were housed in the Fresno County jail, where conditions were deplorable, and at the Industrial Farm. Father Eugene Boyle, who is a Jesuit, and had come to Fresno from the Spirituality Symposium, recalls being in the Fresno County jail for the two week period. "The cell was twenty by thirty, and about thirty of us were in that cell. One of the greatest events we would have in there was the eucharist. I finally induced (the guards to get us) matzas and someone got some Manischewitz wine in to us."[33]

After two weeks, with mounting visibility of the arrests and pressure on Fresno County, all of them were released on their own recognizance. At nine p.m. they were released at the Fresno County Courthouse where hundreds of farm workers greeted them. At a mass and meeting in front of the courthouse, Father Boyle told the farm workers, "This is the greatest number of religious persons ever jailed in the United States."[34] And he was not even counting the 500 strikers who had been in the Fresno county jails.

"It was one of the most significant events of my life," Sr. Rose Cecilia recalled. It had been very hard for her to be without privacy and to have physical freedom taken from her. She remembered spending a lot of time on her upper bunk, just to be a little away from so many people. But the experience expanded her understanding of inner freedom. "When I left I was so grateful for (the experience)."

Hartmire remembers that the people who resented the jailing were those who chose *not* to be arrested. He said, "They took the 'easier' path and were resentful. The others should have resented the long stay in jail but they rejoiced in the experience."

A trial date was set, but charges were dropped before the trial was held.

In Levy's book, Jerry Cohen, General Counsel for the UFW, spoke of the consistent nonviolence of the strikers. "The vast majority of the arrest cases were dismissed. Most of them were for violating an injunction or for unlawful assembly. There were a few assorted charges—like people would throw dirt clods, several threw rocks, and there were some in for assorted scuffles. But when you think that 3,589 people were arrested, I think well over 3,400 of those were clear First Amendment issues and had nothing to do with even alleged disturbing the peace or anything like that. So it was an amazing performance by the farm workers. They really kept their cool when they were attacked."[35]

That summer the UFW lost almost all of its contracts, and two UFW members were killed. Nagi Daifullah, an Arab member, was killed by a policeman. Juan de la Cruz, a long-time UFW member, was shot and killed by a strikebreaker. There seemed to be no justice that summer, only endurance. The helpfulness of Church support people on the picket lines, in the jails, raising money, and bringing food, was fully repaid by what the supporters witnessed and learned from the farm workers. Supporters sacrificed for a day or a week or two. They were well aware that the strikers were on the picket lines everyday. Some strikers were arrested multiple times. And in going out on strike they had lost their source of income, knowing that the harvest comes only once a year.

Jack Ahern, a Catholic layman who was executive for the San Francisco Commission on Social Justice, was out on the picket lines that summer. He summarizes well the rewarding experience for most supporters who were involved that summer. "I thought I was going to help these people . . . But here were people who were taking every kind of risk, who had cut all kinds of shackles . . . for what they believed in. And here was I, who had not cut hardly any shackles . . . So it was a great experience for me, in terms of liberating me from a lot, and changing my attitude and behavior. It was like a conversion experience."[36]

CHAPTER 3

The Farm Worker Movement
Comes To the Cities

*Often only talk results when a person with
social concern wants to do something for the
underdog nonviolently. But just talking about
change is not going to bring it about. Talk
just gives people an out.*

Cesar Chavez in *Autobiography of la Causa*

AN OLD JEWISH WOMAN in Venice, California, was being interviewed by the late anthropologist, Barbara Meyerhof. The old
woman was in a hurry to leave for a Spanish class. She mentioned
that after class she was going to pass out boycott leaflets in front
of a store. Dr. Meyerhof asked her, "Do you enjoy that work?"
She snapped back, "Who could enjoy standing in a parking lot
on a cold day, arguing with ignorant strangers? You don't do
these things to enjoy. It has to be done. That's all."[1]

The UFW boycotts between 1965 and 1975 provided unique opportunities for millions of Americans. People who felt they were
making no headway on other important social issues found they
could make a difference on this issue. People were frustrated and
confused by our continuing war in Vietnam, by a civil rights
movement in which many white Americans could no longer find
a place, and the inner and outer blocks to progress for the

women's movement. The farm workers came to the cities welcoming the participation of all kinds of people, rich and poor, men and women of every color, religious and nonreligious. People who didn't want to give up everything to work for justice could give two hours a week to leaflet, or could refrain from buying grapes, Gallo wine, or head lettuce. People who would never have been confrontive and daring on their own behalf were surprisingly bold on behalf of farm workers.

The issues were so clear. Farm workers were the poorest of the poor in a land of plenty. Eighty percent of farm workers in California were employed by corporate agribusiness. Some of these giant agricultural corporations were multinationals that were involved in Vietnam and in land takeovers in Third World countries. Agribusiness was keeping the people who brought us food poor and hungry. Agribusiness had defended itself from the accepted requirements for all other workplaces, toilets, water, dependable work hours, vacation time, Social Security withholding, and protection of health. For most Americans the issues in the farm worker movement were not confusing because they dealt with life's basics.

The boycott staffs in the cities were run by or included farm workers. The very people the struggle was about were available to us. They would give us first hand, specific information of what had happened to them and others. They would come into our homes and churches and tell their stories. We left such meetings knowing a human being with a name, a family, a history. And we cared what happened to that person. No meeting ended without giving participants a range of ways to help: pledging not to buy the boycotted item, giving money, pledging time to leaflet, donating food or housing for boycotters, having a meeting in a home, joining the boycott staff for a summer, a semester, a year. As former UFW organizer Marshall Ganz said, "The program, the articulation, the committment of the people (in the UFW)," were powerful and attractive to supporters.

The nonviolence and the sacrifices of the UFW were compelling. They inspired people with ideals and refreshed the jaded.

The UFW introduced people to a way of working for change that was not new, but was largely untried. Nonviolence and sacrifice were coupled with a tightly-reined strategy that could change quickly to exert pressure where it was needed.

In this chapter I'm going to tell about what some people in the cities did to support the boycotts and legislative campaigns and what it meant to them. I will also talk about farm workers and others who became part of the volunteer staff, working long hours for board and room and $5 a week (later raised to $10 a week). I'll say something about organizational support for the boycotts, and finally, some of the legislative battles that occupied the boycott organization from time to time.

SOMETHING FOR EVERYONE TO DO

It was the Christmas season of 1965. My close friend, Louise Jongewaard, and I were standing in the night cold handing leaflets to customers asking them to help farm workers by not buying any Schenley liquors. Louise had told me she wouldn't let me leaflet alone at the nearby supermarket. She had made the most gorgeous and heaviest picket sign in history. It had colorful lettering and artificial grapes cascading from the top. We took turns holding the sign while the other gave out leaflets.

We were both members of a nearby church that had lost a lot of members over the civil rights issue. My husband was one of the pastors. Of course, a wealthy member who had stopped attending our church because of its pro-civil rights activity had to come shopping that night while we were leafleting. She refused to take the leaflet.

Neither Louise nor I had previously done anything so public on an issue we cared about. We had worked in our congregation, attended meetings, written letters, voted. But standing on the public sidewalk asking strangers not to buy Schenley was new. I was thirty years old. We were both mothers of young children, and were married to professional men, with homes in the suburbs. In all outer respects we were very conventional. But we both cared about justice. And on the weight of our trusting relationship with Chris Hartmire, we were willing to participate in a type of public witness that was for us unconventional.

Chris Hartmire, as Director of the California Migrant Ministry, had taken responsibility to try to get some people out in front of stores at this key season to ask shoppers to help farm workers by not buying Schenley liquors. Christmas for liquor is like harvest time for grapes. I was just one person on his list of church folks in Los Angeles who might help with the NFWA's first boycott. At the time, I didn't think about the long list of calls he was making. I was living in my own private reality. It was years later that I understood the important role he played in recruiting church people and in other ways supporting the boycotts.

THE FIRST BOYCOTT—A RANDOM EFFORT

In an interview with Jim Drake he recalled the situation of the strikers in late Fall of 1965 and how the Schenley boycott got started.

Chris had sort of turned over the treasury of the Migrant Ministry (to the NFWA), I think. Anyway, we were still feeding people, just living day to day. The grapes had been harvested. I remember that cycle year after year after year, when the leaves began to fall from the Emperor grape vines and you knew that was another season we'd lost. Now comes the pruning, and you can't do anything about the pruning. Then you have to wait for the budding. And then you have to wait for another harvest year.

So what do you do in between? . . . The first year we didn't know what to do . . . I had suggested the Schenley boycott . . . My only experience with boycotts was reading about the Birmingham Bus Boycott. We had all these picketers around. If we tell them all to go back to work or leave the area, we'll never get them back. So around November, Cesar said, 'O.K., Jim, if you think it's a good idea and you think you can do it, why don't you put together a national network and we'll send all these students and all these kids out all over the country and we'll start a boycott of Schenley liquors.

I thought, I've really got myself in for it now. I don't know what the heck I'm doing. But I went to Chris and he either borrowed a thousand dollars or something, anyway he came up with a thousand dollars. He said, 'Here's a thousand dollars and you can organize a boycott with this thousand dollars.

We had rented a labor camp south of Delano. It was mosquito infested and was sinking into the mud. There was an old barracks which was filled with donated food. And there was a little kitchen where we ate interminable menudo. And there were two restrooms, a men's and a women's. So I asked if I could have the women's restroom for my office. I was told 'sure'. So Richard (Chavez) built a desk over the toilet. And I just moved in there. There were no windows, so I put an airwick up to take out the odor.

And I would sleep in there. I still lived in Porterville, so I wouldn't go home at night. I put a phone in and decided, 'I'm going to spend the whole thousand dollars on the phone.' I started calling all over the country—this civil rights thing, and that group. And I'd call people who sent contributions. I'd call up somebody who had sent us five dollars. 'If someone comes (to your town) could they sleep at your house?'

We got everybody together one cold foggy night. 'We're going to start a boycott. Who wants to go?' We had all these kids from Berkeley. We had two teenagers from Mills College, or someplace up north. I remember they said, 'We'll go.' And I said, 'O.K., you're going to New York City.' We started sending these kids all over the country.[2]

REACHING TO FLORIDA

As Jim Drake and others were phoning around the country one of the people called was Rev. August (Augie) Vandenbosche, then Director of the Florida Migrant Ministry. This was his first contact with the farm worker organization across the continent in California. He remembered a phone call from somebody in California to say that Schenley had a tank car of wine coming into Jacksonville, Florida, and could he help keep it from being unloaded? Without knowing so much as who the caller was, but having heard about the organizing going on in California, he got to work. Vandenbosche had excellent ties with union people and civil rights activists in Florida. So he contacted some of these people and they got in touch with people in Jacksonville's power structure. The wine was not unloaded.

This first boycott work in Florida grew into a dynamic support network that has involved Church Women United, denominations, university people, union people and political figures in that state. A few years later after the boycotts had some successes, the UFW was able to get a contract covering citrus workers at the huge Coca Cola citrus groves in Florida on the rumor that the UFW might start a boycott of Coca Cola.

The one contract in Florida had a ripple effect. "Every time Coca Cola signed a new contract with the UFW, the rest of farm workers (in Florida) got a benefit. It filtered down into the system in Florida. It increased the picking rate, it increased the sense of identity on the part of farm workers, even though they weren't part of it. It gave a voice for farm workers. It gave an opportunity for farm workers to rally to one another's needs. And that's just with one contract," Vandenbosche said.[3]

INVOLVEMENT OF CATHOLIC SISTERS

"Asking people not to shop at the store was the hardest thing for me," Marilyn Schafer recalled. She had been a nun teaching high school in San Francisco when she first got involved with the farm workers. "You were really asking people to be inconvenienced." She remembered how helpful it was to picket a store with a farm worker. It was a reminder of why she was out there on that parking lot doing this uncharacteristic thing that became characteristic for her and hundreds of other Catholic sisters.

Marilyn Schafer's first contact with the boycott organization was in 1972 when all the boycott staff was working to defeat ballot Proposition 22, a state initiative measure introduced by

California growers which would have severely limited organizing by the farm workers. But the UFW used this diversion from the boycott as an opportunity to educate a lot of new supporters about the conditions of farm workers and why they were struggling for change. Marilyn Schafer was one of those recruited. She attended a "No on Prop. 22" rally and met Cesar Chavez and Sister Mary Jean Friel who was traveling with him. It made an impression on Schafer that this nun was working full time with the UFW. She became a link for Schafer.

The next year Schafer took about nine high school students with her to La Paz, UFW headquarters in the Tehachapi mountains. They stayed a month, the students doing manual labor and Schafer doing office work.[4]

When she became director of her community's Social Justice Secretariat in 1974 she was informed about and committed to farm workers' organizing. Now she was in a position to be of great assistance to the UFW. Not only did she have this job with a large, progressive community, but was asked to be on many Roman Catholic and ecumenical boards and committees. She saw to it that information about the farm workers and how people could help got disseminated. When people get personally involved they are likely to help for a long time, and you never know what key people they may become.

VOLUNTEERS WHO WERE ALMOST LIKE STAFF

"Boycotts were extremely important. It put pressure on the grower and everyone could participate in it. A perfect organizing tool. People could help even without letting go of their money." This was the reflection of Ralph Kennedy, another stalwart supporter whom the Migrant Ministry could always count to respond. Kennedy was an engineer at North American Aviation in the early '60's, and a rather recent Presbyterian, having been out of the Church for a number of years. Kennedy was among the 44 arrested in the Fall of 1965 in Delano and the one lay supporter.

He and his wife, Natalie, organized leafleting in Orange County for a long time, "It seemed like years. It became part of our regular life." Later when the UFW sent boycott staff to Orange County, they often lived with the Kennedys.[5] They are part of a continuing support group called Orange County Friends of the Farm Workers in a county that is considered one of the most conservative in California.

A Way to Express Anger and Love

Orange County Friends of the Farm Workers has been extremely effective in organizing support for the UFW's boycotts and legislative campaigns. Jean Giordano is another leadership person in the group. In 1985 she came on the staff of the NFWM. In an interview, Jean talked about her twenty years of active support for farm workers in a conservative metropolitan area. For her it had been important as a way of being in touch with the scattering of like-minded people in the area. It has also been a way for this gentle, caring woman to express some of her anger at indifference to suffering and injustice.

Jean Giordano initiated many efforts that ruffled the feathers of people in Orange County. She tells the story of when the UFW sent a large group of farm workers to her county in 1976 to work on Proposition 14, farm labor legislation the UFW had initiated. Friends of the Farm Workers was trying to find housing for the workers. She decided to have a small delegation visit the newly appointed Catholic Bishop and request housing. The Bishop made it clear that no farm workers could be housed in church facilities, and what's more, no leaflets could be distributed on any church property in the Diocese. He then sent a letter to this effect to all priests in the Diocese.

The Sisters of St. Joseph of Orange were long time supporters of the farm workers. Giordano appealed to them for housing, since religious communities own their own property, so they aren't directly responsible to the diocese. The Sisters thought it over briefly and decided the workers could be housed on their campus. As it happened, the Bishop was enjoying their hospitality on the same campus. He was living there and had temporary office space as well.[6] There was a twinkle in Jean Giordano's eyes as she retold this story.

DETERMINED WOMEN

Women were important to the boycotts because they did most of the shopping. There are wonderful stories of inventiveness of women who wanted to help the farm workers. One such story was published in *El Malcriado* June 1966 complete with photographs.

The story was from Chicago where there was a confrontation between women shoppers at a large Co-op grocery market and an official from S&W Foods, which was being boycotted to put pressure on DiGiorgio Farms, the parent company. The women, as both consumers and owners of the Co-Op, were going through the store removing all the S&W cans from the shelves. They were filling shopping carts with the cans and then putting leaflets on them telling other shoppers about the Delano strike and the boycott of S&W products.

An S&W official happened to come into the store at this time. "He got furious at the women, tried to put some cans back on the shelves, and finally, in desperation, shoved a loaded shopping cart at one of the women, who was seven months pregnant. She was knocked to the ground. Police soon arrived and escorted the S&W official out of the store." The store manager helped the women take the rest of the S&W cans off the the shelves, leaving 59 feet of empty shelf space.

Other women were as determined with the mundane task of weekly leafleting. Lynn Ransford was a young teacher with two small sons. She lived in Los Angeles, and around 1970 she learned through the NFWM of the need for volunteers to pledge some time each week to leaflet with the farm workers at stores. She committed two hours a week for an extended period of time.

"It was terrifying, one of the first lessons I had in discrimination. I was labeled 'one of them', and was called derogatory names. It was painful to find myself for the first time a member of a stigmatized group. I was terribly hurt to be regarded as unworthy to be spoken to." At first she took her sons with her, then stopped because she didn't want them to be subjected to abuse. She often leafleted with a farm worker, which helped. Still, "many people did not want their lives interfered with in any way . . . The more middle-class Anglo population was the most rude, especially men. I had always been treated with respect and courtesy (by men)."

Why was this busy young professional woman willing to take the time and the abuse involved in leafleting? She had known about conditions for farm workers since childhood. She grew up in an outlying part of Los Angeles which had been agricultural at the time. Her best friend in elementary school was a farm worker child. Ransford was one of six Anglos in the school.

She was supportive when she heard about the Delano strike and subsequent boycotts and stopped buying grapes as soon as the boycott started in 1967.

Ransford's refusal to buy grapes caused a family confrontation. A member of the family felt sorry that her little boys were being deprived of grapes. Whenever they went to visit her she had grapes for them. Finally, "I had to tell her I did not want her serving grapes to my boys. She was going to have to respect my feelings. There was no way that I could teach them the values important to us if there was not some kind of consistent stand taken."

Another reason she participated in boycott work was to support nonviolence. "I was so disturbed by the violence of the '60's. I felt that this was one of those rare nonviolent pushes for change

that we should support if we were ever going to see change . . .
Also I wasn't alone in my sympathy and protest . . . There was
an organized way for me to become involved."[7]

SOME CAN ONLY BE CAST OUT
BY PRAYER AND FASTING

Strikers who went out on the boycott and their supporters sometimes fasted to show their seriousness and to call themselves and
others to a rededication to nonviolence. We must not lose sight
of the fact that a nonviolent labor struggle in the United States
is very unusual.

Three boycott staff were sent to Canada in 1968. In 1969 their
campaign was focused on Loblaw's chain. "They were being very
stubborn," according to Jessica Govea, who was director of the
staff. At Christmas that year they decided to hold an eight day,
around the clock vigil at one of the Loblaw stores. Marshall Ganz
from the staff fasted for the eight days. "At the end of the vigil
on Christmas Eve we went over to the office to celebrate Christmas Eve and watch Marshall break his fast. Someone had made
Marshall some mushroom soup . . . The Ontario Director of the
Public Employees Union came over and said, 'Do you think I
could have a bit of that soup?' We said, 'Of course, Keely.' His
name is Keely Cummings, a very dignified white haired gentle-
man . . . It turned out Keely had been fasting the whole time too,
in solidarity with Marshall and the struggle. He had been doing
it without declaring it or anything."[8]

In August 1973, the Teamsters had raided the UFW contracts,
and there was violence on the strike lines. Chavez called on supporters across the country to join the strikers in a three day fast
for nonviolence. People participated all around the country.
Several of us in my congregation in Los Angeles fasted together,
meeting each day at lunch time for prayer and reflection. One of

those who fasted was James Stewart, pastor of the church. I asked him why he did that. The first reason he thought of was that I had asked him to.

"People I cared for and trusted shared that invitation. It was a cause I believed in. And it was an opportunity to immerse myself in a way I had never done before in a time of reflection. I was also curious. I had, of course, heard of fasts and fasting, but had never done it before. It really did merge issue out there and internal life in a potent way."[9]

At the end of the third day hundreds of fasters had a candle-light procession through downtown Los Angeles to Pershing Square where there was a rally and a kind of ecumenical mass to end the fast.

TAKING A BIGGER STEP

Hundreds of people took a bigger step than those that I've described. The supporters did a lot, and it was important that people boycotted grapes and whatever else, that people contributed their time, money, homes, that people fasted, prayed and vigiled. But none of it would have worked if some people had not become full time, unpaid staff.

Hundreds of people joined the UFW staff between 1965 and 1975. I'm going to use the experiences of several people who had strong religious backgrounds to show some of the reasons people joined the staff, what it was like for them, what effect it had on them.

Farm Workers on Staff

Farm workers were the backbone of the staff, beginning of course with Chavez, who was a farm worker until he joined the Community Service Organization. Many strikers agreed to join the boycott staff and travel to the cities when there was no longer any practical purpose served by maintaining picket lines around fields. These farm workers were a powerful influence on sympathetic people in the cities.

One such striker was Raquel Venegas. She was from Mexico where her family still lives. Raquel was working at West Foods, a mushroom farm in Oxnard, California. Raquel's work on the boycott staff falls outside the decade we've been examining. But her experience is the same as many farm workers from '65–'75.

Raquel came from a very poor family in the state of Durango. She only went through sixth grade and later got training as a nurse's aide. She came to the United States speaking no English and got the job at West Foods when she was 21. There was a UFW contract at West Foods when she went to work there. Karl Lawson, a UFW staff person for Oxnard helped acquaint her with what the Union had to offer. A labor dispute arose over the company's dangerous pesticide practices. As a result, the UFW decided to boycott Dole bananas, a label of the parent company, West Foods. In January 1982, Raquel agreed to go on the boycott.

With her very limited English and her sixth grade education, Raquel was given a week's training and sent to New Orleans. In an interview in the Spring of 1985 she told me that it was rough because people in New Orleans didn't know about the boycott or the UFW. "There were some religious sisters at a place called Hope House. They helped a lot. They let us work out of their office. They helped us with the work, contacts, names and addresses. They helped us with a lot of miracles." Raquel was in New Orleans only two months.

By the time I got done, everybody knew the UFW; everybody knew about the farm workers and what the boycott was all about. And we had supporters from the sisters, from all kinds of convents, from schools, and also from the college. At the college we made friends with directors of the programs. We liked them a lot.

We went to doctors' offices, lawyers' offices. We went to everyone's house. They were amazed because they couldn't believe that an illegal alien, Mexican, who couldn't speak well the English or understand it, was doing the boycott in such an area where they didn't know much about the boycott.

She was transferred to San Francisco with two other farm workers.

The two guys working with me were great. They didn't speak any English, but somehow they let the people know what they were doing. We organized picket lines, we checked out the produce with the managers at the stores. If they didn't cooperate, we right away called some people over and had a picket line at their store. They didn't like that. But we loved it. The people did too. The people were very enthusiastic about it. It's surprising. When you don't know about the Union, when you're just working there by yourself, you don't believe that people like to do picket lines.

We received help from a lot of churches. A (Catholic) brother helped us out and gave us hospitality for the whole time we were there, a month and a half. We worked out of their house and they had a telephone they let us use. We asked (people) for donations, for food, because the Union doesn't pay.

When asked whether she has been changed by her work with the UFW, she laughed and said she didn't think her family knew she was the same person. She had been very quiet. Now she feels confident to stand up for people's rights. She agreed to be the union steward for the cooler and packing shed at West Foods, and she loved helping the workers defend themselves if there was a legitimate problem.[10]

Farm worker men and women who could not speak English, some of whom could not read or write in any language, who had little experience with anything outside of farm work, made the boycotts work in cities all over the continent. Marcos Munoz headed the boycott in Boston. "He couldn't read, so he memorized all the directions." Eliseo Medina spoke very little English at the outset. He became an outstanding organizer and an eloquent speaker in English. Maria Saludado was one of many young women who left their families, a daring break with tradition, to go on the boycott. She went to New York and many other cities with almost no money, and maybe only one name and phone number. Maria, as so many, asked for the help she needed with the few English words she knew, and took cold and lonely places and made in them communities of support for herself and for those who helped. Any one of them could organize the socks right off of you and make you glad they did.

Students On Staff

Starting with that first boycott, many students became boycott organizers. Most of them were college students. Some would come just for the summer. And some would stay. There are people on the UFW staff, as I am writing this, who originally came as students on vacation. Others came for a limited time and didn't stay with the Union, but the Union has stayed with them.

The UFW has stayed with Dr. Wooden (Woody) Garvin, now a Presbyterian minister in Pasadena, California. In 1973 he was a seminary student and needed an internship. Garvin had heard a bit about the farm workers' movement and about the National Farm Worker Ministry's support of the UFW. He made the necessary arrangements to be a NFWM intern and was assigned to the Los Angeles boycott. When I met with him recently he enjoyed telling me the funny, surprising things that happened during his internship, and how much it all meant to him. His internship started in the hectic summer of 1973.

Reporting to work was going to this dilapidated old home, filled with people who basically were just in the process of living. And as the morning meeting was beginning, there were children running around and wild-eyed people. I felt like a real foreigner in a foreign land at that moment. I was really embarrassed and shy.

Our assignment was, 'Here's a map of Los Angeles. Somewhere off to the east of this map is a place called the San Gabriel Valley. God bless you.' We had a little pad of paper and someone told us, 'We think that there is a Quaker organization out there. So when you get to Pasadena, call them and see what you can do. And here are the names of two people who send us money.' And that was about it.

So we all got into this car, about six people, an old Dodge Dart with the hubcaps off, with boycott and strike signs sticking out of the trunk, which was tied shut with a piece of twine. And off we go to the San Gabriel Valley. We drive into (Pasadena) and Bobby (De la Cruz) gets out and uses the phone. And the slow process of getting inside the community begins. Actually, Bobby had previous experience.

We had six people and it grew to eight or nine. And all these were volunteers, in the absolute sense of the word. They were everything from sweet Hispanic people who only knew a couple of words of English, who didn't know anything about being in the city, and really didn't know quite what it was they were a part of. They were farm workers who had decided to jump in the stream and off they were, going over the rapids. Then there were seminary students involved and college students doing a project. Then there were people who came probably because the farm workers were the only people who would take them in, people with deep psychological problems and misfits. They were given a home and a purpose. So we were thrust together. There was a family-like atmosphere.

They started each morning at 7:30 with a meeting at Harvard House and worked though the evenings six days a week. Garvin did a lot of organizing at churches.

It was my first real experience being in an ecumenical environment. My own roots and background were very fundamentalist and conservative. I was still working through fundamentalist prejudices, which were not in my operative mode but were questions to be answered underneath the surface. I can remember engaging in these fascinating theological discussions with nuns on the picket lines . . . about should Christian witness include evangelism or not. And out of my background . . . it was like you should say, 'Please help the farm workers and don't shop in this store, and do you know Jesus?''

There was essentially no training for anything. It was 'Try this.' and 'Go do that.' 'Find a place to work out of and go do what you need to do.' 'Find some money to support wherever you work out of.'

Garvin, as all other UFW volunteers, had to ask people for whatever help was needed. He depended on Church people and groups to help with money, food, and a place to work. He also called on church people to arrange meetings so he and the others could tell their story and ask for support including coming out to the picket lines. He remembers that many people offered a full range of help. Others wanted to know about the "myths": Chavez's castle in the Valley, and Cadillacs, and wasn't he a communist? "Actually it was very delightful, because they were easy to answer, because you could just tell the truth. That's always powerful," said Garvin.

The UFW policy of integrity made a deep impression on Garvin. One incident stood out in his memory. Jim Drake was the Los Angeles boycott director at the time. His second marriage took place that year at Harvard House. Everybody on the L.A. boycott came to the celebration. Some of the behavior was rambunctious, but "nothing that college students wouldn't feel O.K. about anywhere." But the next day at the morning meeting they were called on the carpet and told they must live their lives by the highest standards. They were given the choice that they could live by high standards or they could leave. There wasn't going to be any tolerance for stuff that might be damaging to the work of the farm workers. At a follow-up meeting, Chavez came and talked about keeping their hands clean. "When you go to people and you ask them to give you something, you have to go with your hands clean."

Garvin commented that, although the farm worker issue was one of the most controversial issues of the day, the UFW could literally engage anyone about it if the staff came from a place of real integrity. "That has the Gospel written all over it." He made the application to the Church's life. "Because the Church has avowed a very radical call to reorder human society, then the Church, to the degree that it works at that message, has to come from integrity. The standards the Church lives by have to be immaculate."[11]

Professionals Join Staff

I mentioned LeRoy Chatfield in the first chapter. In 1965 he was a Christian Brother and principal of a Catholic High School in Bakersfield, California. He had first met Chavez in '63 through the National Catholic Social Action Convention in Boston. He stayed in contact with Chavez, inviting him to speak to classes and involving high school students with farm worker kids in the summers. In the Fall of '65, Chatfield enrolled in a doctoral program at the University of Southern California in Los Angeles. Almost immediately, he was getting phone calls from Delano asking him to organize truckloads of food for the people who had just gone on strike in the grapes. "I raised some food and took some people up there to help on the picket line. Then it was just a few days afterward that I decided that if I could be of help there I should do that. So I left the Christian Brothers, I left USC and I went to work with the Union."

Chatfield worked with the UFW for eight years. I asked him what kept him working that long. He answered:

It was a very concrete way to be of help to people who needed help. And the issues were straight forward: the rights of workers to organize and have a union. And from the Catholic Church point of view, you could hardly have a more bedrock issue than the rights of workers . . . And there was an organization that was growing and developing that a person could tie into to help. And that was important. It's very hard to go out and do something by yourself. That's why what Cesar did was so unique. It's hard to do something on your own steam and your own resources . . . Working with him and the people around him gave you a lot of support.

LeRoy Chatfield directed many campaigns during his eight years on staff. And he organized support groups in different areas of California.

I got to meet wonderful people, people who were just waiting to be asked to do something. That's a good feeling. You go into an area and no one has ever heard of the farm workers or Cesar, and in a few days, a few weeks, a group comes together around the issue and is very supportive. They begin taking small steps at first, then much larger . . . You might not see them again for six months. Next time they're probably in Delano.

Chatfield was assigned to Los Angeles to direct the Proposition 22 campaign, the Safeway boycott, and the DiGiorgio boycott. He ran a tight ship and was an outstanding campaign director. He was a professional man in a religious community, and all someone had to do was ask him to help. He gave eight years, plus recruiting several other outstanding people who also worked full-time for a number of years, among them Bonnie Chatfield, a teacher whom he later married, and Marshall Ganz, a remarkable organizer out of the civil rights movement.[12]

Nothing can be written about the UFW boycotts without talking about Fred Ross. You remember that Fred Ross started the CSO and trained Chavez. Not everyone who helped with the boycott got the Fred Ross/Saul Alinsky training, but *everyone* learned some of the principles and techniques, even if it was just not to be so damned nice. And I think everyone learned that— learned that, to really care about the poor, one will need to lean on people who are keeping them poor.

Ross told me he figured he had directly trained over 4,000 people recruited from the churches and colleges plus farm workers. He's a very tough trainer and insists on results. And although Woody Garvin started work on the boycott with no training, unknown to him at the time, Bobby de la Cruz had been trained by Ross. In the midst of all the chaos of those years often with several campaigns running simultaneously, and no money, there was a basic kind of order. The full time people were required to keep lists, and mark off everything they did, account for all their time and their sparse resources.

You can travel around the United States today and find people working and organizing in every kind of effort and discover they were trained directly or indirectly by Fred Ross.

Just as Chavez had formed an organization that people could tie into, these full-time people made it possible "to form the contributions of others into something useful."[13]

CONCLUSION

In conclusion, one can see that volunteers and staff helped for similar reasons and with some similar effects on them. People helped because: the issues were compelling, there was something for everybody to do, they were asked, they were challenged, the policies of the UFW for nonviolence and integrity gave people confidence in the organization, and the religious roots of most of the workers were a bond for supporters from faith communities.

The Church was a significant source of volunteers and volunteer staff. Why? Why would a middle-class church which has demonstrated an historic separation, if not down-right antagonism to organized labor, become a source of support for the UFW? The Catholic Church involvement is easier to understand. As LeRoy Chatfield pointed out, there is policy and history there for support of labor organizing. But in reality the middle-class church, Roman Catholic or Protestant has been isolated from organized labor.

The movement has been too complex and too many individuals' decisions have been important to give a simple answer. But clearly Chris Hartmire's work as director of the CMM and, after its organization in 1970, the NFWM, was crucial. Rev. Walter Press, who was Associate Conference Minister with the United Church of Christ, when asked about the surprising relationship between the Church and the UFW said, "I don't know how it could have happened without the Migrant Ministry and Chris Hartmire."

Fred Ross praised Hartmire's work. "Chris was so helpful in helping us uncover people within the churches, not just in California but all over the country. He was spending a lot of his time every year getting ready for summer, when so many people from the Church as well as students could come into our boycotts, which were in all of the major cities and a lot of the minor ones. And without the kind of help that he gave, we couldn't have been nearly so successful. He's just damn good at convincing people."

Ross went on to describe Hartmire's participation in training. "Chris used to come to each training session I put on across the country. After we'd gone through the whole thing, he was the last point on the agenda. He would get up and give a great inspirational talk."[14]

There was this kind of personal work. But the NFWM staff and Board also tracked every important denominational or religious community meeting and worked hard to get boycott resolutions passed. Those resolutions were "worked" by boycott staff as well as NFWM people. Hartmire gives a lot of credit to boycott staff for finding out about regional meetings and chances to get the boycott before Church bodies, and for energizing local people who kept taking the issue higher and higher in their communions. Hartmire observed that, "People fell in love with the farm workers' movement in their local setting. And they made sure *their* church did the right thing on *this* issue." There was a natural flow back and forth between the Union and the Church. There was NFWM staff on the boycott. There was UFW staff that were grounded in faith communities. Working with local Church people was natural.

Strikes and boycotts were not familiar to the Church per se. But justice work, nonviolence, solidarity with the poor were unassailably Church territory. Hartmire showed genius in getting beyond the activities of strike and boycott to reveal to the Church the meaning of the farm worker movement. A later chapter will focus more on this.

People in and out of the Church also helped because it made them feel more powerful. There was so much frustration over other social issues and many people felt they had no way to make an impact. With the UFW they were told, "This is what you can do." And with supreme community organizing skill, modicums of success were produced to keep up people's spirits. A whole generation of organizers learned how to pick the local targets, how to make it fun to make change, how to keep supporters involved, excited, and challenged.

No one will ever be able to count the long-term benefit to society resulting from the thousands of people who worked on the boycotts and who, in so doing, learned how to organize people and make change.

In 1975, the Agricultural Labor Relations Act was passed in California. This legislation was designed to bring agriculture into the twentieth century. It replaces striking and boycotting with a simpler procedure of workers on a ranch voting to indicate if they want to be represented by a union, and then requiring the owner of the ranch to engage in fair negotiations toward signing a labor contract with the chosen union to cover relations with his workers. The UFW threw itself fully into use of this law between 1975 and 1985, dismantling the vast boycott network that had been developed, and making some strong supporters feel lonely and even abandoned. By 1985 the effectiveness of that law had been gutted and the UFW returned to the boycott.

Cesar talking with Sue Miner and Chris Hartmire. Sue was Chris' Administrative Assistant for twenty years and had that position with the two prior Directors of CMM.

Chris Hartmire at UFW's Forty Acres in Delano with church supporters.

Cesar Chavez and Dolores Huerta at UFW headquarters in Delano in early days of the Union. (Photo by Chris Sanchez)

UFW strikers on Sacramento March during Lent 1966.

At the end of his twenty-five day fast, Cesar eats bread. His mother hands him juice, while thousands stand around him at the Delano Park.

Celebration at the end of Cesar's twenty-five day fast in Spring of 1968. Left to right, Dolores Huerta, Robert Kennedy, Andy Imutan, and Jim Drake.

Rev. Howard Matson supporting UFW organizing in Florida.

Unitarian Universalist women supporting the farm workers. Left to right, Toni Wolfe, Bea Berg, Sylvia Berke, Gaye Deal in front of Santa Monica Community Church in 1976.

Police separating UFW strike line from Teamster hired "guards" during tense summer of 1973.

"Fresno Sixteen." A list of religious women in one cell at the Fresno County Industrial Farm in Summer 1973. Courtesy of Rose Cecilia Harrington, CSJ.

Left, Fr. Sean Flanagan, right, Fr. Ed Penonzek on picket line.

Catholic priests celebrating mass at opening of UFW health clinic in Coachella in 1976. Photo by Cathy Murphy of the UFW.

UFW strike line in Coachella Valley in 1973 with United Church of Christ supporters. Photo by Lynne S. Fitch.

"Billboarding" in the San Francisco Bay area for Proposition 14.

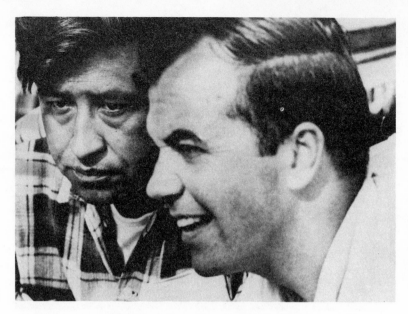

Chris and Cesar meeting in Delano.

The Hartmire family at Thanksgiving 1986 at UFW headquarters at La Paz in Keene, California. Left to right, John, David, Jane, Gordon, Chris, Janie. They all went through a lot for Chris' calling.

CHAPTER 4

Opposition Targets
the Church

"ALL CLERGYMEN, WHETHER LOCAL or those traveling uninvited into a community, who lead, incite or participate in any unlawful behavior or civil disobedience bring doubt and reproach on all men of the clergy . . .

"Be it resolved, by the Executive Committee, acting by direction of the Board of Directors, of the Kern County Farm Bureau, County of Kern, State of California, that all church groups and their governing leaders, redefine their areas of responsibility so that their clergy will refrain from participating in social reform activities in any locality that results in lawless, irresponsible actions that endanger the life and/or rights of citizens."

This statement of the Kern County Farm Bureau was passed unanimously on the twenty-first day of October, 1965, just one month into the grape strike in Delano. The opposition had already begun to focus on Church support and clergy activity in particular. The support of local laity and those from outside the area was less visible and less targeted. In an interview in 1976, Chavez said that in the early days of the strike, the Migrant Ministry was "more controversial than the Union itself."[1]

The first year of the strike, Hartmire and denominational and ecumenical executives who had come out in support of the rights of workers traveled steadily up and down the San Joaquin Valley meeting with angry groups of church people.

Hartmire did little to cool the controversy. He remembered his initial tendency to pull his punches and try to communicate in Valley church meetings where 95-98% of the people were angrily opposed to the Ministry's presence in Delano. "Eventually, I figured out," he recalled, "that *nothing* I could ever say would change our opponents—and that I needed to be as clear and strong as possible for the 3-5% who were with us. Most of them were taking risks for the cause and they needed solid support. Though small in numbers, they were the people who counted in those meetings." He allowed himself to stay in the pressure cooker for months. But he also recognized that, as painful and exhausting as it was for him and other supportive clergy, the controversy was putting the problems of farm workers on every denomination's agenda.

Hundreds of resolutions, in the early days mostly statements of support for the California Migrant Ministry's work, were debated at regional and national meetings. Many resulted in votes of confidence for the CMM. Others, (e.g. the Episcopal Diocese of San Joaquin) condemned the CMM for its involvement in the Delano strike.[2]

The CMM Commission stood squarely behind this new direction in ministry. The Northern and Southern California Councils of Churches also were solid in their support. The denominational organization which took the most heat was the Northern California Conference of the United Church of Christ where the controversy focused on support for the Rev. Jim Drake. At every annual meeting for several years, there was debate over his salary. But the leadership and a majority of delegates were able to maintain a budget item for his salary until 1969. By then there was sufficient national money for the CMM to hire him as Migrant Ministry staff.

Throughout the next several years, clergy in the Valley and some outside the area found their jobs threatened because of their support for the strikers. The embattled support by some segments of the Church for the strike was significant in bringing wider attention to the situation. The controversy erupted into the national press. Pictures of clergy being arrested on strike lines in Delano were shown on television and in the major newspapers and news magazines.

Had the strike been contained to farm workers in an isolated area of Kern County there would not have been national interest, and the strike probably would have had an early death. Who really expected this strike to succeed? There had never been a successful farm labor strike in the continental U.S.[3] as far as redistributing power. Strikes occasionally gained a higher wage for those particular workers for that season but left the basic power imbalance untouched. So when the strike began in the grapes in Delano, people in the community probably thought it would be like all the previous strikes, it would be broken in short order. The most workers might hope for would be a small increase in wages to match the increase AWOC achieved in grapes in the Coachella Valley earlier that same season.

The relationship between growers and workers, the workers' place in the society of the Valley, the use of labor contractors, the way agricultural business was done, none of this was likely to change.

About two weeks into the strike AWOC and the NFWA, the two organizations whose members had left the fields, were running out of money and food. Chris Hartmire got the word out for church people to gather food and bring it to Delano, and they did. He and Jim Drake got the word out for clergy to come to Delano and be present on the picket lines with the farm workers and with Migrant Ministry staff, and some came. Although it was only the Migrant Ministry and some individual clergy and church members helping, many Valley people were incensed that the Church was helping keep alive a strike they expected to die a natural death.

Chavez was putting his mind to work on strategies to keep the strike going and keep up the morale of the workers. The infusion of resources from the Church bought this struggling bipartite strike organization time to mobilize other resources from community and civil rights organizations, as well as from some of the big unions.

Soon people in the Valley were dismayed to find "long haired hippies," "radicals" from the city, "outside agitators" who would defy law and order had come to their Valley. The civil rights movement, the anti-war movement, the student protests had invaded the San Joaquin Valley. And "liberal" clergy were out there with them on the picket lines, at the rallies, and sometimes going to jail. It was a shock.

It was an affront to the way the agricultural community lived its life. These strangers from outside, and some defectors from within, were noisily proclaiming that the way agribusiness did business was unjust and immoral. These strangers were talking about a way of life for people in the Valley, and not just those who used farm labor, but every person who thought things were all right the way they were. I want the reader to understand what a jolt this was to non-farm workers in the agricultural valleys, and why their anger was especially intense toward the clergy.

"They had lived a certain way of life, a certain culture, and no one told them it was wrong for a lot of years."[4] The Catholic sister who was speaking to me was from Fresno, from a family who had been small-scale grape growers. She told me I could not use her name because twenty years after the fact the divisions in her family are not healed. The opposition to the Church's support for the farm worker movement was seldom argued on theological or Biblical grounds. It was a conflict over social values which had long been blessed as Christian. And it was sparked by deep anger that churches—Methodist, Presbyterian, United Church of Christ, and others—"had turned against their own members to support people who didn't even belong to those churches." And it was a fight over who, in the Roman Catholic church particularly, would be heard: members who were poor and farm workers, or wealthy and middle-class members.

Most would agree that the strength of reaction against the Church's involvement in farm labor organizing could be attributed in part to the social context of the '60's. Social rearrangements were being forced by the civil rights movement. Anti-Vietnam War protests pitted youth and some non-youths against authorities. Students were rejecting values and practices of their parents. Women were renewing the demands from the earlier part of the century for equality. The farm workers struggle, in terms of numbers, was minute in comparison to these other movements. But it brought the volatility of social change home to the naturally conservative agricultural valleys of California.

"For those of us from the Valley, it was a very difficult situation. Because we were raised to believe that people like Cesar Chavez must be communist. And that we were wonderful." Sister Marilyn Rudy was raised in Fresno. Her family's next door neighbor was in management with one of the largest farms on the Westside of the Valley. "I heard it all my life: 'These farmers are so wonderful to their farm workers. Why, at Christmas they give them free gifts!' And I used to think, 'How wonderful' never realizing the kind of life the workers lived . . . Living in the city (of Fresno) and knowing the white collar farmers is a very different story from driving in the heat of the Valley and seeing where the farm workers live."[5]

Rev. Karl Irvin is a Disciples of Christ clergyman who grew up in Lake County, California, on a farm where they grew pears and walnuts. At picking season, his family would warn him about the "fruit tramps" who would come to the area to pick fruit. His family felt all right about using the common practice of not providing housing for temporary workers but allowing them to camp out in the orchards while they were in the area to pick pears.

Karl and his wife Ethelyn, who was from a midwestern farm, took up farming too. They wanted to provide better conditions for temporary workers on their own farm and did. "I think fundamentally for us we had some feelings that great advantage was being taken of farm workers."[6]

Allan Grant is a retired dairy farmer, a Presbyterian layman, and for sixteen years an executive with the Farm Bureau, first in California and then the national executive. He was a major spokesman for the growers between 1965 and 1975. He believes in decent wages and working conditions for farm employees. He told me with a good deal of spirit that he knows there are farmers who mistreat their workers and that the workers "didn't have any recourse. And that's wrong. It's just as wrong as it can be."

He believes "Chavez did some good . . . He got farm labor to recognize that they are individuals with the same rights as other individuals in this country. They have the right to a voice and ought to have the right to say what they think about their treatment."[7] But he found the Sixties a distressing time and he did not like having outsiders coming to the Valley to be on picket lines. He reserved his special anger for liberal clergy and Chris Hartmire in particular.

CHALLENGING THE POWERS

As the Union and elements of the Church began mounting an effective challenge to the powers in the San Joaquin Valley, the growers and their friends came back fighting. The growers didn't believe, didn't want to believe, didn't want others to believe, that their workers were not happy. They claimed that there was no strike (even after the State Dept. of Employment certified in September 1965 that there were 23 strikes), that "their workers" were happy, that bonafide grape workers from the area had rejected the Union, that the NFWA and AWOC were simply run by outsiders who were trained organizers, and that growers had a greater concern and respect for farm workers than the either AWOC or the NFWA.

These were astonishing claims, claims made by people who felt their backs were to the wall. But why did they feel so pressed?

Their Belief System Was Being Challenged

The agricultural industry in California had little by little over the years established a belief system which supported injustice and kept business costs down. How could good people, church people, think it was all right to have poor farm workers living like animals in the orchards, with no shelter, no reliable source of clean water, no toilets? One had to believe that they were "fruit tramps," humans of a lower order, people who had chosen these conditions and must like them.

The "fruit tramps" were seen as care-free wanderers with none of the worries and responsibilities of "community people." The first time I ever heard the term "fruit tramp" was twenty-eight years ago. My husband and I had been in Mendota, California, for two or three months, where he was serving the Methodist Church. It was summer and the town population was swollen with farm workers and others there to pick and pack cantalopes. I heard about an old woman who, because of her poverty, was still doing farm labor and was living in a little grower owned shack by the railroad tracks in town. She had been ordered to vacate with one day's notice. Being a naive twenty-three year old I phoned the wife of the foreman. She and her husband were members of the church my husband was serving. I asked if there was something I could do to assist this old woman who worked for them. She dismissed my concern as totally inappropriate and unnecessary since the old woman was "just a fruit tramp" who was used to sudden moves.

Where have we heard these ideas before? "They like their life the way it is." "They're not like we are." Racism from Southern plantation life somehow seeped up in the San Joaquin Valley like toxicity in ground water. Rev. Karl Irvin, a native of the Valley who knows it well, told me, "Racism is rampant. My congregation would grow upset if there was any, even token, thing extended to the Mexican people in the area, because they were not considered on a par with other people." Rev. Irvin welcomed strikers to stay at the church building when they were passing through town on a march. He believes that the negative reaction was because "there were brown people in the church building."

Many Christians in the Valley were charitable to farm workers. But their charity did not challenge their basic belief that brown and black and even white farm workers were of a different order of humans than themselves. Rather, charity made the giver, as Sister Marilyn Rudy said, feel he or she "was just wonderful."

Chavez and the "uppity" Mexicans who banded with him didn't fit the stereotype. Valley residents rationalized that Chavez and his people were "outsiders." As Allan Grant wrote in an article which appeared in *Presbyterian Life* in December 1968, "Until 1962, Chavez worked with the Community Service Organization, during which time he was trained in Chicago under the astute tutelage of Saul Alinsky."[8] He went on to comment that Dolores Huerta, who was vice president of the Union, had been associated with the CSO in Hanford (which is in the San Joaquin Valley) and was also a former trainee of Alinsky.

Neither Chavez nor Huerta had received their training in Chicago nor from Alinsky. The Chavezes set up shop in Delano because Helen Chavez's family lived there. Both Helen and Cesar had grown up doing farm work. So between 1962 and 1965 Helen and Cesar supported themselves doing the familiar work of farm laborers. But the fact that Chavez and Huerta were "trained," that they had held other jobs or positions than farm workers, maybe even that they had been to cities outside of agricultual areas was enough to make them "outsiders."

An entire exploitative system of agriculture was maintained on the belief that farm workers (most of whom were people of color) were different from the rest of us. The strike that began in Delano and was initially shored up by church people was such a challenge to this important belief that it elicited surprising and largely untrue defenses. I don't know if statements disclaiming any strike, and proclaiming society's respect and regard for farm labor were believed by the growers, but they might have been.

"There is no strike in Delano. More than 5,000 of the people who regularly, year after year, have picked our crops, stayed on the job," stated Martin Zaninovich, a Delano grape grower. He was testifying before the Senate Sub-committee on Migratory Labor which had been called to Delano in March 1966 to investigate what was going on. A few days later, Zaninovich gave almost the same address to the annual meeting of the California Grape and Tree Fruit League meeting in San Francisco. In commenting on the march to Sacramento which had just begun, he said, "About 100 so-called farm workers, along with ministers, priests, professional demonstrators and some self-styled leaders started their trek towards the State Capitol in Sacramento. The parade is nothing more than a publicity stunt for the benefit of the news media."

A 1966 growers' public relations pamphlet called "The Delano Story" written by Leslie Taylor claimed, "There is no discord between the farmer and farm worker." Other publications stated that Delano grape growers met often with their workers, and that farmers were more generous with their workers than any other category of employers. The growers had or adopted a sense of outrage that outsiders had taken on a concern for "their" workers. The "Delano Story" says, "The primary concern of the union, clergy, migrant ministers, and their sympathizers is not the farm worker. In fact, they are only doing an injustice to an honored and respected group in our great society—the farm worker."

Talking with farm workers, you get quite a different story. Jessie de la Cruz lived near Delano in Parlier. She and her husband, Arnold, had worked in the grapes for one grower every season for many years. She said she had seen the owner, but he had never spoken with her. Jessie and Arnold de la Cruz joined the NFWA May 1, 1965. After the strike began in Delano, they continued working in the Parlier area. One day the grower came into the field to speak with her. He asked her what she thought of Cesar Chavez. She quietly continued cutting grapes and asked, "Who is Cesar Chavez? Does he work here?" The De la Cruz family became deeply involved with the Union. Their home was the Union headquarters in the Parlier area. About three years later, Arnold had received calls from the ranch asking if he was coming to work that season in the grapes. He had not returned the calls. A few days later, Jessie saw the grower drive up to their house in his pick-up truck. He took a few minutes looking over the house covered with UFW posters and *huelga* flags, and just drove away. They never worked for him again.[9]

Jessie de la Cruz and other farm workers I've spoken with talked about how hard they worked and how little they were paid. They talked about the lack of contact with the owners. (Most farm workers are hired and paid by labor contractors.) And they speak of terrible—and illegal—working conditions: no toilet facilities, no water to drink, inhuman demands for picking speed, personal abuse and degradation by labor contractors and foremen. Growers would personally admit abuses, but they were always in some other area.

The Rev. Charles McLain was one of the first clergy arrested in the Delano area. He and the others arrested with him were held overnight in a Bakersfield jail. The experience was not an easy one for McLain. But what awaited him in his parish in the Los Angeles area was much more difficult. It turned out that two elders in his congregation had brothers who were grape growers in the Delano area. They saw McLain on television being arrested. They were furious. A special meeting of Session, the ruling body in a Presbyterian church, was called to talk with him. The Board of Deacons held a called meeting in a member's home where the host greeted McLain at the door and directed him to, "Sit over there so we can shoot at you." McLain was astonished by the reaction in his urban congregation and the interest of local news organizations in his arrest.

"What I learned," said McLain, "especially for these rather conservative people in the Pasadena area, was that the Church and especially the leadership of the Church and their pastor, should never get this involved in acting out what we say we believe . . . They weren't in touch with their real belief system." He believes that people in this congregation and their friends and relatives in agricultural areas had accepted values common in the society and believed them to be synonymous with Christian values. The conflicts between actual Christian teaching and their value system had remained unnoticed for years. McLain's actions revealed the conflict in an unanticipated way. Many in the congregation, he said, were furious at the publicity focused on them, and communicated that he had no right to involve them in the conflict.[10]

McLain's experience contained some of the major elements of the dispute that arose in the Church over support for the farm workers' organizing. But there were other elements, especially related to the boycotts, that were ethically more complex.

BOYCOTT'S EFFECT ON SMALL GROWERS

"My family was among the small people who got hurt. They were attempting to do the best that they could . . . I watched my whole family deteriorate." This Catholic sister was in her late teens when the Union began the boycott of all table grapes. Her exposures through the Church and especially through Fr. Roger Mahony, who now is Bishop of the Los Angeles Archdiocese, made her sympathetic to the plight of farm workers and the need for organizing. At the same time, her family was suffering from the actions which were empowering farm workers. It was painful for her even after all these years to recount what had happened. She asked me to picture the situation.

"If you could imagine what it was like for a family to be driven apart and some permanent injuries occurring as a result of beliefs. Picture what it was like to be eighteen and have a strong sense of caring for my family and my family caring for me and find myself on the opposite side of something that was causing a great deal of suffering."

Her family decided to sign with the Union in the frenzied flood of contracts in 1970. At that early stage and under tremendous pressure, the Union's hiring hall (which replaced the hated labor contractor system) did not work well. She said her family lost a lot of money "because the farm workers did not meet the terms of the contract. They'd promise X number of workers on a certain day and the grapes had to be picked that day, and they had half of the (workers)."

The bottom dropped out of her family's part of the business. Her father found a similar job with another small company and it folded also. He was without work for awhile with the personal and family tensions that often accompany unemployment. He eventually found work with the city government.

In the meantime, another part of the family negotiated a contract using the arbitration services of Fr. Mahony and stuck it out. That part of the family believed that unionization was right for farm workers. The family split that occurred was permanent. The sister remembered that her cousin was a close friend. They were the same age and car pooled to school each day. One morning she got a call saying that her cousin wouldn't be picking her up any more. She has not seen her cousin for twenty years.[11]

The problems of small grape growers were real and painful. Some small growers wanted to sign contracts but found that local bankers could make it tough to get loans, and other growers were disapproving. The concreteness of the problems and the possibilities for practical interventions by the Church were obscured by those whose worries about "the small farmer's problem" immobilized them from doing anything about the farm worker's problems.

In 1970, the Rev. James Hogue was the Executive for the Sierra Synod of the Presbyterian Church. His synod took in the San Joaquin Valley. He wrote a brief article which was published February 9, 1970 in *Monday Morning*, a weekly magazine for Presbyterian clergy. He was taking issue with a report by a national denominational committee on the agricultural situation. The report favored the consumer boycott. He dealt with the whole enormous struggle by saying that, "Men of faith are in short supply on both sides of this power struggle which makes the theological point for supporting the boycott weak and ineffective. Both sides deal with power and are not concerned with being open to each other as men."

Mr. Hogue went on to speak of the plight of small grape growers and to ask the question, "How can Christians support a boycott in the name of reconciliation and justice which wreaks havoc on so many others? There must be a better way to bring justice to agriculture workers. It makes sense to me that our church would be much more just, moral and theologically consistent if we put as much effort in obtaining national legislation, which would protect the agriculture worker."[12]

Hartmire responded with a letter to the Editors of *Monday Morning*. He noted Mr. Hogue's distance from the actual struggle and pointed out that Synod executives were probably not "empowered to decide who is and who is not a man of faith. And even if they were, Mr. Hogue does not know Cesar Chavez and the leaders of the farm workers movement."

Hartmire went on to tell about meetings between small growers and union representatives in which negotiations were impossible because small growers are "economically dependent on the large producers and their banking allies who have decided to resist unionization at all costs." He challenged Mr. Hogue, as he challenged many similarly concerned church people over the years, to find a way to help small farmers organize just as farm workers were organizing to improve their position to bargain for what they needed.

He concluded his stinging remarks by saying that if Mr. Hogue knew a better way to make needed change, "he should step down from his place of power and help the workers build a more effective strategy. Cesar Chavez and the farm workers . . . have tried all the ways they can imagine to bring the growers to the bargaining table. The boycott seems to be the one disciplined, nonviolent strategy that works."[13]

Even strong friends of the UFW's organizing efforts vacillated on the boycott of all table grapes because of the economic pressure it put on small farmers and on growers not being struck. In August 1968, Hartmire wrote to a Lutheran executive and a supporter of the Migrant Ministry. This clergyman had been trying to come to terms with the consequences of the boycott of all grapes. Hartmire posed his frequent question, "What alternative do the workers have? What can they do against the combined economic power of the table grape growers?'' He goes on to raise the question, "Suppose it takes a boycott like this to bring the industry to its senses but people refuse to support it because of concern for small farmers—what will be the result? We will be back where we have always been with a poverty-stricken and humiliated work force, unorganized and unprotected (and that is not the situation of the small farmers). That will be one result of that form of ethical sensitivity . . . The ethical choices we have are lousy. But I think that we have to make a choice—a relevant ethical choice that will in fact (and not in theory) help workers get a union.''[14]

The Migrant Ministry frequently admonished small farmers and those who supported them to get organized to solve their problems of marketing in the shadow of corporate agriculture. The National Farmers' Organization, which was strongest in the midwest, was doing just that, and they understood the need for the UFW boycott. They did not make a great public issue of it, but many NFO leaders did come out in support of the grape boycott.

The truth is that until a group of people with a problem get organized to solve that problem there is very little that other people can do to help them. Our best efforts will be weak, partial, and will often get misdirected.[15]

Small farmers were not the only ones to lose jobs at the height of the farm labor struggle. There were clergy who had to leave jobs, or chose to leave, because of their sentiments about the organizing effort.

The Rev. Eugene Boutilier was Assistant Pastor at First Congregational Church in Fresno from 1963 to 1966. In July of 1965, before the Delano strike began, he had participated in the Linnell–Woodville March protesting increased rents on dilapidated government-owned farm labor housing. After the grape strike began, he spent a day on the picket line when McLain and others were arrested. He spoke freely about the situation and his view of the dispute.

In November '65, he received a letter from his Christian Education committee directing him "to stop certain activities not consonant with the purposes for which he had been hired." (The actions were not specified.) Boutilier was surprised. This was, as he told me, "a strong, healthy, liberal church." He and the senior pastor had been active in civil rights issues, even bringing Dr. Martin Luther King, Jr. to Fresno to speak. These previous activities had caused no dissension.

Boutilier was worried about the congregation. He said, "It was clear to me that my self-understanding and career in the United Church of Christ was not at risk, but the congregation was."

Then some members of the Board of Directors, ruling body in the U.C.C. congregation, "turneu up the heat" to get him to leave. At a special congregational meeting, members had a spirited discussion of the rights of their pastor to get involved in the farm worker struggle. Boutilier remembered some of the discussion. "One person said that if Jesus were alive he wouldn't be down there and be involved with communists and trouble-makers. Bill Johnson, a friend and the church moderator, was an orange grower and lawyer. He said, 'You're wrong. If Jesus were alive he would be helping farm workers. He would be there all the time. But I wouldn't be paying his salary.' "

Boutilier observed that many growers showed more flexibility on the issue than people reliant on farmers. "Shop keepers, farm equipment sales people and others couldn't afford to appear to be in league with labor organizing." He also felt that many Valley people were not opposed to farm workers organizing but had an "intense fear of disapproval" from others.

Boutilier picked his time to leave First Congregational. Six months after he received the letter and just after Easter, he resigned and went to work full-time with the Migrant Ministry. He wanted me to understand that even with the pressure he received as Assistant Pastor, he loved the job and he loved the church in Fresno. It was clear that he still loves the people he knew there.[16]

Maintenance of the status quo with farm labor was like the bed-rock running the length of the Valley. But the Union's organizing successes caused an earthquake that sent people into a fearful flurry of condemnation and exaggeration.

The Rev. Winthrop Yinger was pastor of a Congregational church in the southern part of the Valley. He had come there in 1963, a young pastor from New England. He had served another congregation in an agricultural area, but knew little about conditions for farm labor. As part of his community service, he joined the board of Friendship House in near-by Bakersfield. Friendship House provided services to migrants and others in the community. Through this connection he met Chris Hartmire.

After the strike began, Hartmire visited him and asked what he thought about the strike. Yinger said he hadn't thought much about it. He accepted Hartmire's invitation to meet Chavez in Delano. He also attended a Friday night strike meeting at Filipino Hall in Delano. "I watched what they did and listened. I got that side of it." Then he decided to visit some farm labor camps. "That's when my mind began to shift dramatically when I saw, not simple poverty, but injustice and deprivation of a kind I had never seen. And I have worked in the slums and in the ghettoes, but this was awesome." He visited farm labor camps in Mendota and one just outside of Arvin, the one John Steinbeck wrote about in *Grapes of Wrath*, and found it the same as depicted in 1940. He said, "I mean, nothing had changed. There were corrugated iron houses and water outside and I don't think there were lights. Just nasty, just rotten conditions."

Yinger continued his research by spending a day picking peas. "I worked my buns off . . . and I made $1.78 that day." He recalled seeing guys selling pop in the field for five times what it normally cost and the workers having to squat in the field when they needed to relieve themselves. He went out several more times and picked beans, tomatoes, and grapes. "People were paid in cash as soon as they brought their crate in and dumped it . . . and no records were being kept (for Social Security or other benefits). Babies and little kids were sleeping in the backs of cars. The other kids who could walk were out in the fields with the farm workers. I knew this wasn't right . . . And I knew that the Church had to make some response to it, because the Church is historically on the side of the weak, and where there is injustice to try and balance it."

He decided he would not use the pulpit to deal with the issue because it's a "monologue with a captive audience." He started Wednesday night town meetings and invited growers, migrant ministry staff and Union members to debate. "I was shocked by the reaction of some of my folks. They didn't want to debate. They said there wasn't another side because the workers were just communists, agitators and hippies." Some of the small farmers in the congregation approved of the UFW's efforts but were fearful of making it known because of social and economic consequences.

An event in the community solidified his support for the Union. A Mexican-American foreman in the area was a UFW supporter. He was fired and given 24 hours to get out of company housing. The man went into town to get his wife and children. While he was in town the house he had lived in and all his belongings were burned. "That turned me over the hill," said Yinger.

He did not push his congregation, but he went out on the picket lines. He tried to continue dialogue in his church. But finally the Board of Deacons came to him and told him that they wanted him to stop praying for the agribusiness situation (in which he included farmers and strikers). He recalled that they told him it was not really "an issue that has anything to do with the Church and we certainly don't want you to mention the farm workers anymore because that is not a Christian issue, it's a communist issue." Yinger told the men that meant a parting of the ways for him and the congregation. The next week he resigned.

He quickly found a position as Director of the Fresno Council of Churches, but continued his active support for farm workers' organizing. Because of that, financial support for that organization dried up and soon he was looking for another job. A supportive professor at Fresno State University arranged to hire him in the English and Speech Departments. Later Yinger returned to pastoral ministry in another part of the State.[17]

Other pastors who did not lose their jobs thought they might and lived through a great deal of turbulence. The Rev. William Dew, a United Methodist clergyman, served two congregations in the Valley and later was appointed District Superintendent for the Tulare area of the Valley. Some of his closest friends were growers and he affirmed that, "There can be a depth of relationship that has to do with how people care about one another as human beings though they may not see eye to eye about social, political issues. They can still . . . understand deeply how those affect human beings and how the Christian community can hold us together in spite of (differences)."

Regardless of his good relationships in the congregation, there was opposition to his support for unionization. Like the other pastors that have been mentioned, Dew was on solid ground as far as official positions in his denomination went. The Methodists had a long-standing position in their Book of Discipline on the rights of workers to organize and seek collective bargaining. And Dew's Methodist Conference held a historical commitment specifically to farm labor's right to organize and, Dew pointed out, it was in line with the Methodist Book of Discipline.

The apex of the opposition in his congregation was a motion made at his local Administrative Board meeting, in opposition to the United Methodist Church's support for collective bargaining. At the meeting, Dew cited the Book of Discipline's paragraph supporting collective bargaining. But the motion passed with about twelve people voting for it, three against and five abstaining. "I had real troubled feelings when it was over. Everybody wanted to go for ice cream to be sure there were no hurt feelings." His wife Mitzi recalled that, "It was very hard for Bill." She remembered when he got home that night saying, "My world is falling apart and they want to take me out for ice cream."

It was a hard time for Dew in spite of the fact that the congregation also voted to raise his salary, which was a vote of confidence in him as a person. He stayed there another year as pastor.[18]

BENEFITS GROWING OUT OF THE CONFLICT

In spite of the turbulence and worry, Mitzi Dew said, "that time was wonderful. It was painful, but it's a wonderful thing to finally have to deal with some really pressing issues. I don't know why it hadn't happened before."

Mitzi Dew especially affirmed the pressure on her to make a personal decision. She commented that as a busy young mother she had not up to that time been called to account in a major conflict situation. "I remember feeling I could not walk the fence anymore. I sure tried." She loved the members of the congregation *and* she supported the rights of workers to organize. She felt that the necessity to think through the situation and take a position was good for her.

Many social issues come to us through the news media or in other ways, but we seldom have to decide where we stand on them. The issue of farm labor organizing and the Church support for it became dominant in the Valley. People had strong feelings about the issue and forced other people to take sides.

Outside the area immediately affected the mechanism of the boycott had a similar effect. People responded to requests to help and called others to account. Church executives and business people and homemakers were checking grape boxes for the union label and personally asking market personnel not to carry non-union grapes. Young people asked their mothers not to buy grapes. Mothers told their little ones that their family did not buy grapes. People reminded their friends not to buy grapes. Normally gracious people reminded their hosts at parties that they should not buy grapes. These kinds of encounters, of course, caused discussion and even arguments. People had to be clear on the issue. People had to respond. "Thank you for telling me. I will stop buying grapes." "Tell me about it. Why should I not buy grapes?" "I think Chavez is a communist and I plan to keep on buying grapes."

The conflict forced people to make a decision and the more people who were committed the more opportunities there were for conflict. It grew exponentially. McLain recalled, "You never dream that you are going to have that much impact on people or that kind of power. But it wasn't my power." He realized the turmoil he created was because of the juxtaposition of long held values and ways of operating agribusiness with another set of values that affirmed new rights for farm workers. And he recognized that the impact he had was predicated on the work, strategies, and risks being taken by farm workers.

CHAPTER 5

Solidarity As Servant Ministry

I would argue that most of the necessary preparation took place because of a basic decision on the part of the California Migrant Ministry to go with the people and be their servants to the limit of our ability to understand and to serve . . . From that stance beside the workers there was only one place to go: into the center of the bracero struggle, local community organizing controversies, and the drive to organize farm workers into a strong, democratic union.

Wayne C. Hartmire

HARTMIRE WAS REFLECTIVE sitting in the living room of his trailer where he and his wife now live at La Paz, the UFW headquarters in the Tehachapi Mountains of California. He was remembering his early sense of the importance of what Chavez and the NFWA were doing. And he was trying to remember where his instinct for the importance of their work came from. He recalled representing the East Harlem Protestant Parish on a 1961 Freedom Ride:

I remember when we got to Tallahassee and they closed the restaurant at the airport, red-necks were beginning to surround the airport, the press all wanted to talk to the Freedom Riders. And I just knew, better than many of the people in our group, even better than some of the older people, that we were supplemental to what the local Black community were trying to do. They were doing it, they were taking the risks, and they were sacrificing, and we were just along to help. About half our group left early because they had appointments or other things. To me it was a scandal. How could you leave? These people go through this every day. How could you leave them until this thing was finished one way or another, until we either got in that restaurant or were arrested?

(He was among those arrested.)

He felt that as a group the Migrant Ministry never overestimated the importance of its role. "This was a part of the strength of our relationship, the Migrant Ministry's and the Union, but also mine and Cesar's. It was never anything (Cesar) had to explain or waste his breath on. That was the way we operated."[1]

The preceding chapters described the Church's involvement with the farm worker movement, its strikes and boycotts. This chapter concentrates on the person and the organization that were most responsible for the Church's involvement. To do this I will look at the idea of servanthood and how it was expressed as solidarity in the context of the farm worker movement.

The idea of serving others arises in a context with a history. It comes out of some concrete experience. There had been the idea within the Ministry that farm workers needed more power over their own lives. Was this a theological idea? The Ministry staff understood it in the light of Biblical justice. It was, and is, about two million farm workers across the country living lives of hard work and destitution while keeping a nation well fed. It was and is about two million individuals whose shiny hopes for who they are and what they might do are tarnished before they ever reach adulthood.

And there was the idea that what Cesar Chavez and the farm workers were doing was important. That anything else the Church was doing concerning farm workers was supplemental and secondary. If the Church wanted to be involved with some important liberation work, it had better find ways to tie in with the poor people who were doing it.

We will first take a close look at these two ideas: that farm workers should have more power over their own lives; and that Chavez and the workers with him were about that important task and should be supported by the Church. Then we will see how they were linked to a Biblical view of servanthood.

POWER IN THEIR OWN HANDS

Doug Still in the fifties recognized that the basic problem for farm workers was not having enough power over their own lives. How power could be built became the question for the California Migrant Ministry. Doug Still and Chris Hartmire attracted a staff committed to the empowerment of farm workers.

Chris Hartmire wrote the following succinct description of the situation for farm labor in 1965:

Farm workers are disorganized, weak and poverty stricken while their employers are highly organized, affluent and powerful. The latter unilaterally make almost all decisions about size of work force, wages and working conditions. They exercise determinative influence in county and city governments. Through a variety of boards and advisory committees, they influence public agencies that are supposed to serve and/or protect the workers.

A lone worker has no chance against this power array and knows it well enough to swallow anger. An affiliated worker will at least get far enough in protest to discover the interrelatedness of the forces opposed to the worker's best interests.

. . . The key issue, therefore, is the organization of workers into effective civic and labor organizations that can deal with basic injustices . . . Given a fair return for their labor and some security in employment, farm workers will buy for themselves and their children the services we want to give them through special programs.[2]

The earliest effort toward empowerment was community organization, with CMM staff organizing farm workers to identify problems and solve them. The idea of farm workers building power was shaping the priorities and job descriptions of the CMM, even as many of their traditional ministries continued.

JOINING HANDS WITH CESAR CHAVEZ AND THE NFWA

As I've mentioned before, CMM staff knew that the main problems affecting the lives of farm workers were job related, but, on the whole, staff felt unprepared to tackle labor issues. Farm workers needed a union. State Migrant Ministries cheered on union organizing efforts as they appeared in California, Florida, and elsewhere. But nowhere on the continent had professional labor organizing been successful in agriculture. The Ministry, with no training in labor organizing, was not about to try it, although Hartmire recalls that they did think about it but "we were ill-equipped and probably afraid of the responsibility."

Enter Cesar Chavez and the National Farm Workers Association (NFWA). The importance of what Chavez and the NFWA were doing was not immediately apparent. When Chavez began organizing in 1962, the CMM didn't drop everything to assist, nor did Chavez want that kind of help. And when the grape strike was called in September 1965, it was called by the AFL-CIO sponsored Agricultural Workers Organizing Committee (AWOC). The NFWA joined the strike a few days later. If CMM staff were looking for a labor organization to help farm workers get contracts, the fledgling NFWA would not seem a strong contender, at least for the near future. Chavez was doing community organizing, patiently building an indigenous farm workers' organization. He hadn't planned for any major labor action for several years.

The importance of what Chavez was doing did not strike the the Migrant Ministry like lightning and cause them to change everything at once. The decision to serve farm workers (the next idea we will examine) led the Ministry toward a growing awareness of the importance of what the NFWA was doing.

Chris Hartmire allowed himself and the resources of the CMM to be available to the farm workers as soon as the strike was called. As a result, other commitments were let go.

The course of events forced us to let go of several other ways of being with farm workers; because of the urgency of the strike and boycott (and the example of the strikers and boycotters) we had no time for meetings with other agencies, with friendly government officials, with people who wanted us to receive and spend federal anti-poverty resources. We let go of dozens of peripheral relationships and 'fruitful projects'. We learned to focus on the people of the UFW movement—on their battles and their needs. It was dangerous because the closer we got the more we were challenged to respond, the more we were drawn into the swirl of the action.[3]

The transition from a Ministry that decided on its own how to help farm workers to one that accepted the priorities of the farm workers' movement took about two years to complete.

THEOLOGICAL ROOTS

What was this servant ministry of the CMM? Basically, it was giving up the authority to decide how to help farm workers and vesting that authority in a farm worker organization. Hartmire points out that the relationship was relatively easy with Cesar and the UFW, and with a less well-organized, less religious group it would have been harder, and with some groups it might not have been sustainable.

Having vested authority in the NFWA, the Migrant Ministry reached out to people of faith, to congregations, committees, denominations and urged them to join the Ministry in this form of servanthood.

Hartmire interpreted the farm worker movement to the Church as a setting in which to act out faith, and as a setting in which faith was being acted out by farm workers. These ideas were on the theological and social cutting edge in 1965.

Sitting in that trailer at La Paz, I asked Chris Hartmire what books or people had most shaped him. His wife called out from the next room, "I can tell you that. Bonhoeffer and the Bible."

Hartmire's Biblical basis for what he was doing and calling others to do was clear and explicit. Practically every edition of the Migrant Ministry newsletter started with a pithy exposition of a passage from the prophets or the Gospels. Of the people I have interviewed, many mentioned those expositions as important sources of inspiration. The influence of these expositions on clergy and laity will probably never be understood because the vehicle was so undramatic. The major themes were justice, servanthood, and the joy that comes from living fully for others.

The influence of Bonhoeffer was implicit. The Biblical expositions and the very work of the Migrant Ministry revealed an understanding of God as described by Bonhoeffer in passages that Hartmire marked and sent along to me because they were important to him. One passage was from "Who Really is Christ for Us Today?" written in Spring of 1944 from prison.

God lets himself be pushed out of the world on to the cross. He is weak and powerless in the world, and that is precisely the way, the only way, in which he is with us and helps us . . . Christ helps us, not by virtue of his omnipotence, but by virtue of his weakness and suffering . . . The Bible directs man to God's powerlessness and suffering; only the suffering God can help. (This is the) God of the Bible, who wins power and space in the world by his weakness.[4]

In the early seventies, the Ministry moved out of a comfortable fifth floor suite of offices in downtown Los Angeles to a nearby store front which it shared with the UFW's Los Angeles boycott staff. The Ministry's sacrifices of its own comforts and "noncontroversial and much beloved"[5] image, as well as its decision to join forces with an embattled group of poor people, fixes in history Hartmire's understanding of the Church gaining power through weakness.

Bonhoeffer is also evident in Hartmire's apparent ease in focusing the Migrant Ministry's work in a secular struggle.

Another passage he marked from Bonhoeffer's 1944 writings was from July.

Jesus calls men, not to a new religion but to life . . . The world that has come of age is more godless, and perhaps for that very reason nearer to God, than the world before its coming of age . . . Jesus asked in Gethsemane, 'Could you not watch with me one hour?' Man is summoned to share in God's sufferings at the hands of a godless world . . . (One) must live a 'secular' life, and thereby share in God's sufferings . . . It is not the religious act that makes the Christian, but participation in the sufferings of God in the secular life. That is *metanoia*: not in the first place thinking about one's own needs, problems, sins, and fears, but allowing one-self to be caught up into the way of Jesus Christ, into the messianic event, thus fulfilling Isa. 53.

A few days later Bonhoeffer wrote:

By this worldliness I mean living unreservedly in life's duties, problems, successes and failures, experiences and perplexities. In so doing we throw ourselves completely into the arms of God, taking seriously not our own sufferings but those of God in the world—watching with Christ in Gethsemane.[6]

Hartmire and the Migrant Ministry staff led thousands of people of faith out of religious settings to be present on picket lines, to sit in jail with farm workers, to hand out leaflets on grocery store parking lots, to participate in farm worker rallies, and to understand themselves to be doing God's work. And the Ministry itself willingly took on the ambiguities of direct work in a labor struggle. The U.S. Church was coming out of a long sleep of religiosity. Books like Harvey Cox's *Secular City* had just come on the market. And many people were eager to experience their faith in a vital, relevant way.

In the eighties, I think we are again seeing main-stream congregations looking wan—bored and boring. One of the blessings of the farm worker movement was that it provided clear, demanding, vitalizing challenges to people of faith. Their beliefs were transformed from liberalism to authenticity. The Christian, separated from people who are struggling for justice, develops only a flabby piety. Such religion is safe but lacks energy. Engagement with dispossessed people tests and strengthens faith. People who virtually had left the Church out of disappointment and boredom entered into this new faith learning-while-doing opportunity and took heart "that the Church might yet be saved", to quote a close friend of mine who had left the Church. The Church needs to remember the value of making demands on members and constituents, and not to hedge in communicating Jesus' call to life.

CONFLICT OVER CONFRONTATION

Other influences shaped the Ministry and the farm worker movement. Surely one such influence was from Saul Alinsky's Industrial Areas Foundation and his premise that powerless people are the ones to be organized to solve the problems concomitant with their powerlessness. Alinsky's organizers had trained most of the Ministry staff. And Fred Ross, a former college literature teacher and one of the organizers on Alinsky's staff had trained Cesar Chavez. Each trainer and each person trained brought something of him or herself to a subsequent style of organizing. But the basic premise of organizing people on their own behalf was not altered. Alinsky was very controversial because his organizing pitted groups of one class against organizations of another class. Because of this, opponents labeled him a communist, an unfounded charge. (The UFW made at least two significant departures from Alinsky's methods. One was to organize middle and upper class people to help the farm workers. The other was to organize farm workers and people to help them on more than Alinsky's narrow definition of self-interest.)

In the sixties, Dr. John C. Bennett, then President of Union Theological Seminary in New York City, was asked to prepare an address giving a theological view of Alinsky's organizing methods in Chicago. The address was called "The Church and

Power Conflicts." This address was of interest to Hartmire and he made copies of it available from the Ministry office.

Bennett began with an assertion "that the political organization of the victims of a situation so that their power can be used to change conditions is an important aspect of Christian social responsibility." Bennett's understanding of the Church's role in organizing victims of injustice was clearly stated later in the address.

The Churches have responsibility to help in the development of forms of power among the powerless in order to counteract the pervasive power of the strong . . . there is a stage in which hidden conflict needs to be brought out into the open. It is a great advance when people who have been powerless, who have been governed chiefly by apathy or fatalism, organize to improve their lot, and this means creating instruments of political and economic power that enable their interests to be felt by the community at large.

At the core of social advance there must be the dynamism that comes from the interests of those who know in their lives the necessity of change.

Bennett's address resupplied the besieged supporters of the poor who were organizing in Chicago and elsewhere. Many Church people were having trouble with confrontational approaches to change: Alinsky's earthy, boisterous sit-ins; Martin Luther King, Jr.'s marches; student protests of the war in Vietnam; Chavez's well advertised strike lines complete with shouting *huelga*. Shouting! People being dragged off to jail! The invasion of our grocery stores by energetic leafleters imploring us to shop elsewhere!

These were an affront to many middle and upper class Christians afflicted with what my husband calls "conflict phobia." Normative congregations in the early sixties were marked by niceness, which at some level of consciousness or unconsciousness helped preserve the status quo which served the people of those congregations rather well. (I count myself in that group.) Niceness as a style of being and relating was the outgrowth of a hope that people were reasonable and that reason was informed by righteousness.

UNDERSTANDING RECONCILIATION

What church people wanted (want?) instead of conflict was to *reconcile* parties with a disagreement. This was usually envisioned as bringing the disputing sides together for a reasonable conversation at a board table or over lunch. I remember a man who was participating in a Sunday morning series on racism at a suburban church. A local example of racism was being discussed as a case study. When the time came for discussion of how the problem could be solved, he wanted to take the offending city official to lunch and explain the error of his ways.

Behind this example was that longing for reason to reign, but a failure to see that it is reasonable to guard one's power and privilege if one's view is not cosmic. It's a verity widely ignored that no one gives up power freely. The poor see perfectly well how power operates. The middle class tend to be more blind about power realities because we are the beneficiaries of the status quo.

Middle class church people were also confused between mediation and reconciliation. The Church can mediate—if asked—between fairly equal and consenting parties. In the farm labor struggle there was no possibility of mediation until the farm workers had developed enough economic clout that the growers would consent to meet with Union representatives. Negotiations between workers and growers was a basic change in the way agriculture did business. This change meant that reconciliation between growers and workers could become a possibility.

Hartmire in his paper, "The Church and the Emerging Farm Worker's Movement," quotes Dan Dodson who said, "Teaching change of attitudes accomplishes little unless and until the social structure is changed."[7] Hartmire went on to add that "the best mission education takes place in the context of crises and that changing structures can set (people) free from old patterns of thought and old economic forces to think new thoughts and dare new deeds for the sake of (others)."[8]

So the Ministry set out, of necessity, to help middle class church people become more realistic about the pre-conditions for reconciliation, and to do some mission education experientially in the midst of the farm labor conflict. Those experiences helped people to see that the deep cleavages between farm workers and their employers came out of a gross power imbalance that spilled over into most facets of community life in agricultural areas using farm workers. The message was that only parties with some equality of power can and will negotiate. The Church's responsibility is to bring the weight of its power to the side of the poor and oppressed in order to tip the scales toward equality and justice. That message must be taught to every new generation. That requirement of faith must be brought afresh to the Church in every season.

HARTMIRE'S PERSONAL EXAMPLE

"Eight of the workers had joined the picket line that morning. They lived in the DiGiorgio labor camp and were worried about going back on ranch property to get their belongings and collect their pay checks. Late in the afternoon Cesar asked Father Victor Salandini, a Catholic priest, and me to accompany him and the workers back to the cabins." Hartmire remembered that it was June 24, 1966. They drove onto ranch property in a large station wagon. About one hundred yards in, there was a road block with a truck, six or seven armed guards and a couple of dogs. Hartmire and the others were ordered into the truck which was completely enclosed. It was summer and very hot there in the Borrego Springs desert east of San Diego.

They were held, most of the time in the truck, until about 10:00 at night. Then they were turned over to San Diego County sheriff's deputies who shackled their wrists to their ankles, chained them together with their arms crossed, ordered them into station wagons and drove them to San Diego. They were booked, strip searched, and held in jail overnight.

The trial was held in a rural area near Borrego Springs. "It was a classic Red scare trial," according to Hartmire. He said it was a jury trial and the prosecution played to the jury with, "If you don't stop communism here, God knows what will happen to us." The workers were acquitted. Chavez, Salandini and Hartmire were found guilty of trespassing and fined $250 each.

Hartmire never played up arrests, but the workers and many church people knew he never asked people to do anything he wouldn't do and probably already had done. For farm workers, there was no doubting he was with them unequivocally.

Another example of Hartmire's leadership for servant ministry was a 21 day fast in 1969. The grape boycott was in its second year, pressure was being focused on Safeway grocery stores. Safeway is the largest grocery chain in the world and had refused to stop buying grapes. Joe Serda, a striker, was in charge of the Los Angeles Boycott. He was discouraged. He and Chris Hartmire decided to do a water-only fast in front of a Safeway store. They picked a store in the inner city of Los Angeles. Hartmire recalled the experience.

They were nice people, almost all poor people. But it was a nasty looking parking lot with no visibility. News reporters would only come if they were given direct orders by the station manager. It was hot summer, kids going by licking ice cream cones all the time. I said to Joe, 'We could just die here. No one cares. Look at those ice cream cones.' Then Jim (Rev. Jim Donaldson) and other people would organize a really neat service on a Friday night, and we did get some publicity on that.

Then Joe got sick and began to get cramps. He got scared and his wife got scared. They wanted to end it. So I think we used the occasion of what turned out to be false negotiations to end it.

It was 21 days of water only. Nothing done in love in the universe is lost, but that was close to it.[9]

What Serda and Hartmire didn't know was that their sacrifice was intensifying people's participation on the boycott in other places. Everyone who knew them felt compelled to leaflet more hours, to write to Safeway, to do whatever they could to get Safeway to stop selling grapes so that Chris and Joe could eat again.

These deeds gave the idea of servanthood personal authenticity. But Hartmire's day-to-day way of relating was what was most often mentioned by denominational executives and pastors I interviewed. Rev. George M. Wilson, who had been a Presbyterian pastor in Palo Alto in the 60's and 70's said that Hartmire's "clarity, directness, and absence of rancor" were important to him, along with the absence of any judgement that others were not doing enough or that the opposition was evil. "(These qualities) provided a bridge, a link so others could identify with Chris."

Dr. Clifford Crummey who was Executive of the Northern California Church Council from 1968 to 1972, said that "People like Chris and Cesar were part of my reeducation. The nice personalist theology I learned at Boston Theological Seminary just wasn't adequate for dealing with the issues."

Dr. Crummey had to worry through a lot of controversy himself, but he was remembering Chris Hartmire's weeks and months of seemingly endless confrontations and challenges in the San Joaquin Valley between '65 and '70. "Few people could have carried out what happened. And Chris did it. On the strength of his long involvement—this didn't happen overnight. And Chris didn't use strong tactics, it was all out in the open. I suppose he's capable of getting mad, but in these sessions (with church people in the Valley) he just carried it off so wonderfully. He had done a lot of homework."[10]

Dr. Richard Norberg, as United Church of Christ Conference Minister for Northern California during the 60's and 70's, was in frequent contact with Hartmire. His integrity and experience were important to Norberg.

Chris was just invaluable in that whole movement as far as the Church was concerned. I don't think we would have been able to understand all the ramifications of the farm workers' movement. It would have been another issue. But because of the traditional tie for so many years with the Migrant Ministry in the former, more traditional role—that was still there. Plus Chris' own charisma, his own integrity that commended him so much to us . . . We knew the kind of sacrifices he was making in his own personal life.[11]

He went on to remember a continuing and galling problem that I, as an organizer with church people, encountered often. Churches have a certain pace of activity with weekly worship, monthly meetings, regular office hours, program materials which arrive from denominational headquarters at dependable seasons. This ordinary pace was in stark contrast to the frenetic pace of the farm worker movement. At any given time, there might be sixty or seventy strikes going on, at least one major, nationwide or international boycott, some law suits, demonstrations being planned, negotiations going on. The Union developed an impressive information network to keep track of statistics on the effect of a boycott, nationally, or in any given city, state, or grocery chain. The Union leadership was constantly strategizing.

With so much information coming in and so much going on, the Union would switch tactics quickly and often. So just about the time that a Richard Norberg had gotten the word out to the congregations in his area to, say, boycott Schenley liquors, the boycott would be switched to S&W canned goods. Then he would have to explain that Schenley was now negotiating and S&W was owned by DiGiorgio, and DiGiorgio was this giant agribusiness corporation that also owned thus and such and refused to negotiate and there were these incidents that happened on one of the several DiGiorgio farms.

This was not easy and it was frequent. Steady might be the better word. Norberg remembered:

We leaned very heavily on Chris, I have to confess, sometimes rather blindly. And it wasn't just me. I and other denominational leaders discussed this on several occasions. 'Would they work out their strategy and come tell us what it is' . . . At times I was quite frustrated, frankly, because the strategy of the farm workers would shift. And would have to shift so quickly in order to do what had to be done. But just when we thought we were on the same wave length, and we were trying to get our churches to understand, when we were zigging it would look like the farm workers were zagging. I would call up Walter Press and tell him to phone Chris Hartmire and find out what was happening . . . We trusted Chris and we trusted the farm workers . . . (But) we couldn't always understand why the tactic was changed and what was now being asked of the churches. It was difficult enough to get support . . .

Chris was very patient trying to explain to us, but beyond his explanation it was Chris who was saying, 'This is a good thing to do.' And I know Walter (Press) and other denominational leaders felt he made the meaningful difference.[12]

I bring up these observations about Hartmire's personal characteristics not only because they were important to the total enterprise, but because he was demonstrating the fruits of the Spirit: patience, kindness, forbearance, and a trusting attitude that showed itself in a fairly consistent cheerfulness. Anyone hoping to give leadership in movements for justice and a greater experience of God's *shalom* needs to attend to the inner person and to the humanity of personal interactions. Trying to do social good in a shoddy way is not effective for long.

WORKER-PRIESTS AS EXAMPLES OF SERVICE IN SOLIDARITY

Several people on the Ministry staff took assignments with Chavez's NFWA from the beginning of the strike in Delano. After two or three years virtually the whole staff was working directly with the Union. They were working with farm workers to organize and run the strikes, and organize support for boycotts in cities around the country.

They worked for subsistence support—what they actually needed for housing, food, clothing, and transportation, with a few dollars extra. In 1972, over the objections of the NFWM Board but at Hartmire's insistence, the Director's salary was put on the same basis.

The Worker-Priest Program underwent significant changes from its inception in 1966 when CMM staff were teamed with farm workers, earned their living (except for a small CMM stipend) doing farm labor, lived in a farm labor community, and did organizing in the community organizing style of discovering the expressed needs of fellow workers. It evolved in response to the actual needs of farm workers organizing.

But integral to the program at all times was the personal witness of living with and serving poor people in struggle.

DISAGREEMENTS

Not everyone on the Migrant Ministry staff agreed with the servant ministry style they had practiced. And some supporters raised questions too. Objections centered on two issues: how best to offer individual and organizational gifts in an effort to make social change; the importance of enough distance from a movement to be able to criticize objectively.

On the first issue, Ministry staff included well-educated, theologically-trained people with skill and experience as communicators and leaders. For some staff there was little opportunity to use these skills. The UFW was making the strategy decisions, and farm workers were scheduled to address groups and interpret the movement to Church groups as well as secular. The Ministry backed up Union personnel. Some Ministry staff spent months and years typing letters, answering phones, and in other ways assisting. Only when Ministry staff were assigned to direct boycott work in cities far away from California were they expected to exercise leadership. Some staff felt in retrospect that this constituted a false understanding of servanthood, because they were not offering the full range of their gifts in the service of farm workers. Jim Drake recalled:

It was Chris's idea and it was my idea. I don't think it was ever Phil's (Farnham) idea very much. And it was never Dave's (Havens) idea. But we would just sort of literally do anything that the leadership wanted us to do. If they wanted us to raise money, we'd raise money. If they wanted us to be picket captains, we'd do that. This later led to a debate within the Farm Worker Ministry as to whether or not we are to exert any kind of leadership in terms of values, and I don't think that we ever resolved that. When I got a little nervous about Synanon stuff,[13] it was too late, because we were part of the woodwork. We couldn't really stand in judgement in any way. We couldn't exert leadership. We were absorbed into this role of just being useful. Which now I believe is a corrupt theology, to limit your true usefulness.

. . . I don't think we should ever make the same mistake, that because we're white we can't be leaders. We were taught that basically, by the radicals of the Black Movement of the '60's. We didn't learn that from the Bible.[14]

When asked about Drake's point of view, Hartmire said, "There's a lot of truth to what Jim says. We gave up a kind of indefinable independence. We couldn't have it both ways, being as close as we were and part of the movement and an objective outside force making valid moral judgements. We chose to 'sin bravely' in order to be as useful as we could be and were." On the issue of where this way of practicing servanthood came from, Hartmire stressed that it did not come from the Union either. He and the staff developed it in the midst of the strike, seeing what needed to be done and "how to be there as usefully as possible."

On the issue of giving up objectivity from which to influence Union decisions, Hartmire observed that, "By being part of the necessary 'woodwork' the Ministry exercised more influence than it could have done from a distance." He went on to observe, "We were more influential than, for example, the National Conference of Catholic Bishops or the Executive Council of the AFL-CIO, for two reasons: our voices and values were there in the inner circles (though not always strong enough); we were useful enough that our views were considered implicitly and explicitly even when we weren't there. Having said that, however, it would also be a mistake to overestimate our inside influence."

Several former UFW staff people thought that the Ministry was too close to the Union. They thought that the Ministry's virtual integration into the life of the Union made it impossible for the Ministry to be prophetic and corrective when there were apparent injustices to Union staff. One former staff person was honest to admit that he had been glad for the Ministry's practical, everyday usefulness. It was only when he had a personal problem with the Union that he wanted the Ministry to be more objective. As a matter of fact, the position of influential, objective outside critic was almost non-existent. Even faithful supporters usually found themselves closed out if they tried to debate Union policy or decisions.

Monsignor George Higgins, working with the Catholic conference of Bishops, was one of the few who was able to maintain a prophetic stance in relationship to the Union as well as the growers. When the Union leadership seemed out of line in negotiations or in dealing with Union personnel, Higgins felt it appropriate to "speak truth to power" there as elsewhere. His occasional disagreements with Union leadership have never ruptured the good relationship he enjoys with the UFW.

Monsignor Higgins and the Catholic Conference of Bishops probably have too much power for the UFW to feel free to write them off. But Higgins also does not write off the Union when he feels it has gone astray. "I was not surprised when Cesar made what were, in my opinion, some mistakes. But some of his followers were (surprised). You become disillusioned when you hold up ideals that can never be realized."

Higgins reflected on keeping some distance from the UFW:

I always thought that it was healthier for me to be very supportive of (Cesar), but to be my own man. Because once your credibility is lost it's hard to get it back. If people say, 'You're only doing that because Cesar wants you to do it,' that won't work . . . I can see that there are some people who may feel that it's their vocation to put aside everything else and serve Cesar, serve the UFW. That's one role. But it was not a role I could play.[15]

Higgins not only had a significant role in negotiations with growers, but also with key figures in the labor movement. The UFW has maintained a rather separatist role in relationship to the rest of the AFL-CIO and has gotten in trouble over it. Higgins helped other union leaders understand the UFW and some of its positions. He feels he could not have mediated for the UFW with the labor movement had he not been seen as independent of the UFW. However, the UFW might never have survived to 1970 if some in the Church had not thrown themselves into the struggle.

The landmark disagreement with the Union, which was referred to by many as when they stopped helping, occurred in July 1977 when Chavez visited the Philippines. The Filipino members of the UFW had urged Chavez to make the trip and Chavez had been promising to go for a long time. Andy Imutan, a former UFW Board member, arranged the trip through the Philippine Department of Labor. The Marcos government saw a good public relations opportunity in Chavez's trip and planned an occasion to present Chavez with an award. The occasion took place, the award was given, and the Marcos government made sure the international press had the story. News of the meeting with Marcos caused consternation among Church supporters who were protesting imprisonments of dissident church leaders and other Philippine government practices.

By the time Chavez returned to the United States, he was awash in criticism. People were urging him to make a statement condemning Marcos. He stonewalled it. From his point of view, he had made a trip his members had wanted him to make. He had traveled to another country as the guest of their Department of Labor. He had not intended negative and embarrassing consequences. And he was not about to allow people outside the Union to dictate what the UFW and its leadership would do. In this respect, the Philippines trip was no different from numerous other decisions which had offended labor unions or other organizations. Many supporters from churches and political groups stopped helping after that trip. Maybe they would have stopped anyway, especially since there was less for supporters to do by 1977. But their unassuaged anger, their inability to have reconciling dialogue—which many tried to get—marked the end of their support. The Ministry agonized about the trip and provided information, but did not go public with its concerns.

Hartmire agrees that the Migrant Ministry lost its objectivity. But he asked, "(If we had kept greater distance) what use would we have been?" He maintains that the key to the Ministry's work was to be in so close that the staff knew and understood the pressing, rapidly changing needs of the movement. Union leadership could not have afforded time to keep explaining things to concerned church people on the periphery of the action. The Ministry, by integrating itself into the movement, served the movement directly with the energy of its staff and by interpreting the movement to less involved church people. It was because of those explanations that church executives, pastors, and laypeople knew how to help and felt confident that what they were told was true and accurate. Jim Drake and other Ministry staff playing useful roles inside the Union made that work.

Supporters of the farm worker movement whether in California or three thousand miles away in Florida or New York were given access by the Ministry to detailed and continuous information on strikes, boycotts, and negotiations. Jim Drake and other staff would feed information from inside the movement to Hartmire and he would conscientiously write down dates, times, names, actions and report them to the wider Church using the Migrant Ministry Newsletter and hundreds of fact sheets. Hartmire produced fact sheets on every important action of the farm worker movement. Ministry staff in boycott cities and with other assignments across the country also produced articles and fact sheets.

Hartmire believes that the Ministry's closeness to the Union was essential for effective servanthood. And as he pointed out, "We never claimed to be the whole Church and the whole Church was never in danger of becoming too close."[16]

Perhaps it was good that some parts of the Church maintained more distance while the Ministry intentionally gave up distance and objectivity. The real problem, I think, is when all the institutions of the Church remain removed from a justice movement, involving none of their people directly. If the Church has none of itself invested, it cannot bring the resources of the Church to the aid of dispossessed people in struggle. If the Church only gives a little money and some advice, when things get hot the Church is likely to bail out. The main reason the Church stayed involved with the Union was because it had part of itself deeply involved.

HOW STRUCTURE CAN AFFECT MINISTRY

"The main structural issue for me," said Hartmire, "was that we were free to do what we did. Free to get that involved. There was decision-making freedom. And by getting involved directly we inevitably pulled in a whole big chunk of the Church's life, first in California then in the nation."

The history of the Migrant Ministry is a history of searching for forms that could bring resources from the Church to the service of farm workers. In 1965, the CMM was a state migrant ministry relating to a local strike and finding ways to channel support to the strikers. By the time the strike in Delano became a national boycott, it was understood that this was not a local event. Many of the grape growers, and later lettuce growers, being boycotted owned properties in other states. Some farms were owned by major corporations like Schenley, Tenneco, United Brands. The boycotts, to be effective, had to be national. It was felt that the Church needed a ministry that could reach out to the Church nationally for support for the farm workers, even though the ones getting contracts at that time were only in California and Florida.

Many, but not all, state migrant ministries agreed and were glad for the formation of the National Farm Worker Ministry. Some state migrant ministries became part of the new NFWM, like the

Florida Migrant Ministry which merged with the NFWM in 1975. Some retained their own identity but became members of the NFWM Board. Others resisted and felt encroached upon.

But whatever the state ministries chose to do, in 1971 the National Farm Worker Ministry was formed as a related movement to the National Council of Churches (NCC). Church Women United, also a related movement, was a model for the NFWM, which wanted a relationship with the NCC without their control. The NCC was actually glad to have the relationship with little responsibility for this radical, sometimes troublesome little ministry.

So the structure that was developed in 1971 gave the NFWM secure ties with the denominations, a freedom to relate to religious bodies not members of the NCC (Roman Catholic orders, Unitarian Universalists, Jews, among others), freedom to set its own course, raise and spend monies as seemed appropriate to Board and staff, and to continue a tight relationship with the United Farm Workers Union and the just developing Farm Labor Organizing Committee (FLOC) in the Midwest.

This new, flexible structure had the advantage of a long history of ministry with farm workers and interpretation to Church people. So there was trust among farm workers and prepared, caring people long related to the Ministry, whatever its name was. Servanthood had always been its mark and solidarity in service was its new expression.

February 9, 1986 Sharon Streater was ordained to ministry in the NFWM. Pat Drydyk, OSF, the NFWM Co-Director, gave the charge to Sharon.

We . . . call you to servanthood among the farm workers who are struggling for justice and dignity . . .

Jesus, by his life, showed us the importance of living at-one-with the oppressed and the marginalized. It is the servanthood of Jesus to which we call you.

To be among farm workers experiencing their powerlessness without giving up hope.

To be poor voluntarily so that the meagre resources we have can be used in the struggle for justice.

To listen to the farm workers and respond to what they ask you to do in their efforts toward self-determination.

To go where they ask you to go, becoming truly a migrant minister yourself.

To open your heart in love and compassion and courage to all , in this nonviolent movement!

To give of yourself, your life, even unto the cross, accepting the death that comes when we love deeply.[17]

The National Farm Worker Ministry may not have found the perfect organizational form or the perfect form of servanthood. But it soars high above the often mundane life of the Church. It has tied its fate to that of farm workers in the tough job of organizing in a resistant industry. In so doing, the Ministry tends to be visible when the organizing is visible, and invisible when the media do not care to focus on UFW and FLOC strikes, boycotts, negotiations, contracts, and services to their members. But the NFWM continues its presence with farm labor and its life within the institutional Church.

CHAPTER 6

Remembering, We May Learn

> *Some things you must never stop refusing to bear—injustice and outrage and dishonor and shame. The Church bears them all too patiently.*
>
> William Faulkner

EMPOWERMENT. What does it mean for people to become empowered, poor people, women, people who have been dispossessed on any grounds? Farm workers and many of their supporters felt more powerful and were more powerful because of their experiences with the Union. How that empowerment took place and how it changed people is the most important lesson to be learned, remembered and applied in new situations. Chavez told this story about empowerment:

The workers want to do something. And you know damn well it's wrong. They want to strike and you know that they may not win the strike. You're not sure if a strike is the best thing. But they want the strike. And you better damn well help with the strike, no strings attached . . . That's your commitment . . . It doesn't matter if it's right or wrong. What matters is they want to do it and they need your help. They need the organization to help them. And that's where organizations, unions, get into trouble, because the leadership begins to make those adjustments because 'they know best.' But let me tell you my experience. Even if you go and lose that strike, but you help them, they are with you.

Chavez went on to give an example. He recalled that some other union leaders advised the UFW not to let the workers negotiate contracts. It was the business of lawyers to negotiate contracts, they said. Chavez and Dolores Huerta recoiled from this elitist advice because of their community organizing training. They decided to have workers participate in contract negotiations. After all, workers knew the issues that were important to them, and direct involvement and decision making would be empowering experiences for them.

On the first contract we negotiated, the workers were getting 75 cents an hour. They wanted $3 an hour. We knew they weren't going to get it. But the workers met and voted for this big increase. So Dolores and I let them go for it. We made our proposal to this seasoned, experienced labor lawyer who was representing the grower. He looked at the proposal and then handed the workers his calling card and said to phone him when they were ready to negotiate. There were about twenty people on the negotiating committee. I didn't say anything. Nobody said anything for about twenty minutes, just a lot of throat clearing. Then they asked me what they should do. I told them that they could go back on strike, do nothing and just go home and forget about the union, or scale down the demands. They learned fast and we got a contract.[1]

Why should the Church or other institution turn over its social action agenda to a justice movement? Not because the dispossessed know better than anyone else what needs to happen, although sometimes they do. But because people who have been beaten down need to know that others believe in them, respect them, will stand behind them as they organize to make humanizing changes. The Church has tremendous power to support the poor when they are in struggle.

In Jesus' stories of the Kingdom, it was those with compassion for the suffering people, the wronged, the dispossessed, who would be saved. Jesus affirmed society's peripheral people. In the Kingdom parables, the master's servants crowded those folks into the banquet, into the wedding feast. Those were the white lambs who were surprised to find themselves at the right hand of the master, being honored. We can never go wrong when we keep company with people who are returning dignity to the dispossessed.

One of Mark Day's stories illustrates how the Union put power in the hands of its members so that they might exert some influence over their own lives. In Summer of 1967, the Franciscans, under Father Alan McCoy's leadership, had sent a young priest, Mark Day, to minister in Delano to the farm workers. The workers had felt quite abandoned by the local priest, an old man who wished only to preserve his good standing in the community. Fr. Day was there only a few months when old Bishop Willinger, responding to complaints, sent word that Fr. Day was to leave the Diocese. Young Fr. Day obediently left, knowing that the Bishop was soon to retire. After his retirement, Fr. Day returned. Complaints were again lodged and the new Bishop Manning sent word again that Fr. Day was to leave.

Chavez was angry and called a meeting to strategize about what they could do. They decided that first Fr. Day should go and talk with the Bishop. If that failed, a second step was planned. Fr. Day met with Bishop Manning, but he was unyielding. As soon as the priest had left, a group of about thirty women from the UFW arrived to visit the Bishop and ask that Fr. Day be allowed to stay in Delano. Bishop Manning made the mistake of leaving his door open and all of the women went in to his office and sat down on the chairs and on the floor. "He had no idea of the power of these women," said Day.

As the day went on the Bishop's staff sent in Fr. Louis Baldonado, a Franciscan, to calm the women down. Then they sent in Monsignor, now Bishop, Mahony. But the women persisted, Day recalled. The Bishop had to go out to a confirmation and while he was out Helen Chavez, wife of Cesar, sat at the Bishop's desk. They had no food except one candy bar. Helen Chavez cut it in little pieces on the Bishop's desk.

When the Bishop returned, the women were still there. Rachel Orendein asked the Bishop, "Bishop Manning, why can't Fr. Day stay in Delano?" He replied, "He can't because I'm the Bishop and God speaks through me." She responded, "Well, I'm just a poor farm worker, but God speaks through me too."

Bishop Manning finally agreed to let Fr. Day stay in Delano, but the women were not satisfied with an oral agreement. They insisted that he put it in writing, which he did.[2]

EMPOWERMENT AND LIBERATION FOR MIDDLE CLASS SUPPORTERS

The farm workers never talked about liberation theology, but they demonstrated it. The liberating power they demonstrated inspired others who in more hidden ways felt peripheral or who felt impotent as they struggled with destructive social forces. The farm workers' nonviolent action program did not drain away the time, energy, and resources of supporters as many volunteer efforts do. Gifts returned to supporters.

Many middle class women were inspired by the farm workers to try themselves out in new ways. Nellie Kratz described herself as "very much a family person, a minister's wife. I never was involved in any social issues until the farm workers, although I was interested in peace work. My only involvements (with social action) were through my husband." Her husband died in 1960. Two years later, she took the position of Associate Regional Minister for women's work with the Disciples of Christ, Northern California Conference. In 1965, she was ordained to the ministry. As part of her job, she served on the California Migrant Ministry Commission. And for a period of time she was a representative to the Northern California Council of Churches. The Council was a key organization for confirming or denying the CMM's new direction in ministry.

Chris Hartmire remembers Nellie Kratz in this new role of denominational leader "among all those men." "She had an unconscious tenacity and insisted on being heard for the sake of farm workers." He recalled a meeting of the Council where they were considering a proposal to support the grape boycott. The

Council itself was quite supportive, but these denominational leaders kept thinking about those who supported the Council and did not support the farm workers' strikes and the boycott. "The chair didn't want to deal with Nellie anymore, but she would not sit down. She just stood there quietly," Hartmire recalled. Her tenacity forced them to be as aware of farm workers as they were of the opposition in the churches. The Council voted to support the boycott.

When I asked Nellie Kratz about that incident, she laughed and said she remembered it and remembered leaving the meeting with the chairman, her friend Bishop Millard. He told her, "You should go into politics."[3] I don't know if it was true for Nellie Kratz, but I know that many women were assertive for farm workers on the road to becoming assertive for themselves.

In the mid-1960's, Catholic sisters were predictable. They wore habits and they entered a limited number of vocations: teaching, nursing, traditional social work. Many felt called to break out of these limits, but it was difficult to do. Sister Marilyn Rudy recalled that time for her community, the Sisters of St. Joseph of Carondolet, the CSJ's. She says that the farm worker movement provided a unique opening for new vocations. Nuns from different religious communities were persistent and successful in getting permission to work with the farm workers. "It laid the groundwork for other kinds of work," she said.

Marilyn Rudy recalled that Clare Dunn, a CSJ in Arizona, went on to be elected to the Arizona State Legislature. One of the two Bishops in Arizona refused to grant Clare permission to run for the seat. A group of the sisters, encouraged by organizing techniques they learned from the farm workers, petitioned their Superior to overrule the Bishop and give Clare permission to run for office. Their Superior finally acceded when Clare told her that running for this position was a matter of conscience. The Superior didn't feel she had the right to overrule a woman's conscience.

CSJ's as well as nuns from other religious communities found inspiration from the farm workers for their own liberation. Marilyn Rudy told about a retreat for forty or fifty of her sisters which was held in Delano, an unlikely retreat spot. "Anyone who was at the retreat at Delano will tell you they trace back a change in their lives to Delano." It was about 1973. The women spent one weekend, sleeping and meeting in a church hall. They did movement expression and told their stories. "We told where we were and what our dreams were." There was a strong affirmation of each woman's experience. "We felt it most appropriate to have the retreat at the center of the farm worker movement. They had been the hub or core of our strength for moving in a direction that said, 'This is what Christianity means to me.'"[4]

Farm workers were "doing" liberation theology before the term was familiar. The personal affirmation and sense of empowerment that farm workers were experiencing spilled out far from the agricultural valleys into the lives of middle class women and men in the cities.

ACCOUNTABILITY

The UFW was (and continues to be) a very intentional and accountable group of people. One Chavez principle is, "People will help. And if they don't it's not because 'people are no damned good'. It's because we did a lousy job of organizing." The farm workers' accountability affected others. One example is Katrina Carter. In the 1960's she was a member of an Episcopal congregation in Los Angeles of which her husband was pastor when the two of them began to get involved with the UFW. The more she was involved the more committed she became. "It was in the farm worker movement that I learned the necessity to hold myself accountable . . . because you were watching people trying to take control over their own lives."[5]

Most middle class church people will squirm out of taking responsibility for justice work if they have no direct stake in it. If not too much is asked, it's all right. But when we contemplate deeper involvement we quickly think about possibly offending people we regularly see at church, at home, at work, or about losing our job, going to jail, getting embroiled in a long fight and not being able to get loose. Middle class people need poor people pulling them into action on behalf of justice and wholeness. Works of love and justice renew our always disintegrating integrity. People who were blessed and renewed in their work with the farm workers are an important reminder of the rewards of the Kingdom. These experiences enhance our understanding of the Beatitudes.

ANTIDOTE TO RACISM

Another gift of the farm worker movement, available in our present relationships with Central Americans as well as in other relationships, were opportunities to unlearn racism and classism. The UFW provided an antidote, if not a down-right cure, to these illnesses. The UFW had taken on such a mammoth organizing effort and were doing it so well.

Katrina Carter was glad to be trained away from giving patronizing help. "The farm workers didn't let us get away with patronizing actions." There was not a vacuum into which the middle class could rush to take charge. As a matter of fact, Katrina was one of many who said she learned how to organize for change from the farm workers. Some of those lessons didn't start with the UFW but with Saul Alinsky and the IAF. But the UFW spread organizing ideas across the face of the nations and they stuck like peanut butter and have nourished many other movements and endeavors. "Look for the small changes toward the larger goal. Determine the viable issues where you can make change," were some of the lessons Katrina Carter remembered and has used, especially in the peace movement.

When racist and classist ideas are dissembled, then true camaraderie is possible between the poor and the middle class. Many people I interviewed spoke with admiration of the UFW's ability to celebrate in the midst of struggle. Every big and small victory was marked by a celebration. And they were fun. Food, musicians, worship, singing, color were part of the celebrative life that supporters were introduced to in the movement. The shared religious celebrations were particularly important to people.

Middle class supporters were also surprised by the hospitality farm workers extended to them. I cannot count how many people I met with who warmly recalled meals at Filipino Hall. (Filipino Hall was the AWOC meeting place and continued to be used after the merger with the NFWA.) They remembered the delicious food the Filipino brothers and sisters prepared, and how there always seemed to be enough for whoever showed up in Delano. Their hospitality was disarming to supporters who thought they had come to serve. It made it pleasant to think of going back.

GROWTH IN THE SPIRIT

Presbyterian clergyman Charles McLain says that his spiritual mentors were Cesar Chavez and Jessie de la Cruz of the UFW. How did farm workers help church supporters grow in their faith? I doubt that farm workers had that intention. It happened naturally. Supporters would go out intending to give a day or two and maybe even go to jail and would be humbled when they recognized that the strikers had all borne major losses—wages, houses, cars, long separations from loved ones. Supporters were confronted with how little we willingly gave up.

North Americans who are not poor have a strong tendency to believe that every problem has a solution, and we will find it directly and will implement it. It is a life lesson and a spiritual lesson to be disabused of this mindset. The life style of the UFW staff and the strikers was a potent reminder that successes may come but they won't be fast and they won't be easy. Success in achieving humanizing social change lies as much in the process as the ends. The trust and endurance of farm workers and Central Americans evangelize us if we allow for it.

The UFW's decision to carry on a difficult and often dangerous struggle nonviolently taught spiritual lessons to supporters. Katrina Carter recalled that UFW strike lines were her first contact with massive violence. It helped her understand what violence means as well as to test her reserves of self control. Nellie Kratz remembered picketing on a ranch in Fresno County. A truck kept driving back and forth on the road staying as close as possible to the strikers. "We had to keep jumping out of the way," she recalled. After remembering some of these difficult and frightening situations, her summary remark was, "The only privilege I was denied in the farm worker struggle was being arrested."

Many men and women found in the farm worker movement new vocational paths. Augie Vandenbosche in Florida says, "It changed me completely. I was committed to being a small parish minister until the opportunity came to direct the Florida Migrant Ministry." That ministry used a range of his skills and aptitudes that might never have been tapped in a small parish. And through the Florida Migrant Ministry he was able to effect significant changes for hundreds of farm workers who would never have entered a Presbyterian church.

Howard Matson was pastor of a prestigious Unitarian Universalist congregation in San Francisco when he got involved with the Union. When he retired, it was to develop the Unitarian Universalist Farm Worker Ministry. He worked closely and effectively with the NFWM in drawing his denomination into active participation with the UFW. "It was the most important ministry of my career." Besides what he learned, he pointed out that the UFW enabled him to be in situations he never could have been in otherwise, and to come to terms with himself and his principles. These two ideas went together. Picket line violence and jailings were challenging experiences that deepened each person experiencing them. He also affirmed moving pastoral work out of the congregational setting. "The pastoral relationships went beyond denominational lines and became person-to-person, which gave breadth and vision to the whole function of the Church, the whole function of religion, the whole function of the individual as a representative of their tradition."[6]

EFFECTS ON INSTITUTIONAL CHURCH

Now I'm going to turn to some of the long-term effects of the farm worker movement on the institutional Church. Of course, the impact on individuals in the Church has an effect on the whole, but it's harder to measure.

The Consumer Boycott

Perhaps the most enduring UFW legacy from the period of 1965–75 is the boycott as a justice tool accepted by the institutional Church. I have not done a scholarly review of the history of the Church's participation in boycotts, but of the church leaders and denominational executives I've talked to, all remember the UFW boycotts as the first national boycotts their denominations supported.

It was hard getting that support. Chris Hartmire and the NFWM staff worked closely with individual supporters to get innumerable boycott resolutions before numberless jurisdictional meetings, annual conferences, presbyteries, synods, general assemblies. All this took time. Chris Hartmire remembered, "After awhile all of us got the feeling that this issue was going to be around a long time. And if it took the Presbyterians two or three years to make a decision, we would need whatever they had decided to do at that time. And if we needed something faster than that, we would go to individuals, or to ad hoc groups or to Church Women United." So there was a constant petitioning of Church bodies to support the farm workers, and especially to support the boycotts. During that decade, practically every Protestant denomination, a tremendous number of religious organizations and communities and the U.S. Catholic Conference of Bishops had come out in support of the farm worker boycotts.

There has been a significant carry-over to other boycotts: the Nestle boycott to protest Third World infant deaths which result from bottle feeding, the boycott of J.P. Stevens Company in support of textile workers, the Coors boycott to protest discriminatory labor practices, and the Campbell boycott on behalf of Farm Labor Organizing Committee in the mid-west. All of these boycotts have resulted in important victories over injustice. Boycott resolutions by religious bodies, and direct support by the members of those bodies were important in these victories. The UFW with the work of the NFWM prepared the way for these later efforts. The wisdom of LeRoy Chatfield has been spread abroad. "Religion and religious life is an integral part of a person's life. It cannot, and should not be separated just because it is about unions or management, or collective bargaining." If it is about people, if it is about suffering, if it is about injustice, it is about our religious life.

People not directly involved in a struggle are hurt by boycotts. The Church has had to confront that reality. The boycott is not a perfectly honed instrument for justice. But what methods for justice have no unjust side effects? The major issue for the Church was to accept that it had power and to decide how to use it on behalf of the poor. It was a decision to be in a ministry of solidarity as Jesus had been, with people not truly accepted in the religious establishments, and scorned by society. Even Jesus' decision not to avoid arrest and death had "unjust" spillover. His disciples were harassed by the authorities. His family suffered.

As I'm writing this, institutions of the Church, and other private and public institutions are deciding on economic sanctions against South Africa. I hear people saying that economic sanctions will cause blacks in that country and neighboring countries to suffer. There is truth to it. But if we listen to those who are suffering now, they are calling for strong actions, boycotts and sanctions by the people of the world. They tell us that they are already suffering and that these imperfect acts for justice are far preferable to attempts to innocently avoid responsibility for the horrendous acts of injustice by the South African government.

Ecumenism

This book may stand as the only written record of the UFW's contribution to ecumenism. The UFW had no representation on the Committee on Church Unity. But it made a major contribution to providing people meaningful ecumenical experiences which increased the comfort zone for contact between different brands of Protestants and between Protestants and Catholics. LeRoy Chatfield, as a Catholic Brother, had never met a Protestant minister before he met Jim Drake. I had never been acquainted with a Catholic sister until I began organizing with the Ministry. Now I count several as close friends. In the farm worker movement, Protestants found themselves participating in the Mass. Catholics sometimes found Protestant clergy concelebrating a Mass with priests. To say nothing of Jewish rabbis and representatives of other religious practices.

These ecumenical experiences were fortunately timed for Catholics and Protestants in particular. Vatican II was just finishing its work and had dismantled many separatist policies. The Roman Catholic church was looking for ecumenical opportunities. And formal Sunday morning visits with a different church could never affect the bond that people felt having Mass on the picket line while Teamsters jeered at the worshippers or at the end of hours of marching through the Coachella Valley in summer heat. Cliff Crummey remembered taking communion at Mass with the farm workers. In deference to Catholic restrictions, he had often attended Mass but never taken communion. But when farm workers had religious celebrations everyone was encouraged to share the elements.

The thousands of people, both farm workers and non-farm workers, who had positive ecumenical experiences through the UFW are inevitably a force for more open, informed relations between religious traditions.

Religious Work in New Places

Mature Christians must break free of narrow definitions of Church and narrow expressions of religious activity. I saw both happen in the decade of 1965–75. For the first three or four years, Church bodies would only pass resolutions of support for the Migrant Ministry. Later, they became comfortable in supporting resolutions for UFW boycotts and for the Union's nonviolent stance. For the first few years Church people would only contribute to the Migrant Ministry. Later, many became direct pledgers to the UFW. Those pledgers did not abandon their support for the Migrant Ministry but enlarged on it.

The significance of this is that church people were weaned away from confined definitions of their ministry and were emboldened to participate as religious people in secular settings without reliance on worn out forms of evangelism. Woody Garvin's example from his boycott work in Pasadena, California, is perfect. You may remember from an earlier chapter that Woody, coming from a fundamentalist background kept wanting to say, "Please don't shop at Safeway. And are you saved?" The evangelism of being present in the ways we are needed with the poor does not lend itself to tabulation. But if the evangel is the bearer of good news to the hungry, thirsty, homeless, uncared for and imprisoned, then Woody Garvin and all the church people, poor, middle class, and wealthy who have presented themselves on behalf of farm workers and other dispossessed people in the world's unadorned surroundings have been evangels and have served the Christ.

Liberation theologian, Julio de Santiana in the book he edited, *Towards A Church of the Poor* asserts that congregations need poor people in them to keep them in tune with Jesus' understanding of ministry and what the Good News really is. Most main-line Protestant congregations and many Roman Catholic do not have the benefit of having marginalized people as forces in their congregations. The farm worker movement, and other struggles of the dispossessed, brought the voice of those who were suffering injustice into otherwise complacent congregations. It created a presence in the minds and experiences of the congregants that keeps before them the need to respond to suffering humanity.

The farm worker movement affected the whole Church in the United States in special and remarkable ways, challenging, enriching, and renewing it. The dissension that occurred was an inevitable part of the process and will always occur when the Church takes the part of the dispossessed. The spiritual benefits to the Church far outweigh the deficits. After all, who among us would want to reshoot the concluding segment of the ministry of Jesus with Jesus as a pleasant old man beloved by all?

STILL BEING ASKED

The Church is lucky that it is still being asked for help. The Church plays the smiling innocent often enough that it surprises me that people with serious need still ask. Yet the pleas come to us from the homeless in the United States, the anti-apartheid forces in South Africa, women around the globe struggling to be seen for who they are, children in destitution, refugees on every continent, farm workers who continue along the road to justice, and the people of Central America. Some respond and are blessed.

Recently, a priest in Los Angeles celebrated twenty-five years of ministry. Fr. Luis Olivarez is pastor of a largely Hispanic congregation in Los Angeles. Cesar Chavez was one of several people who spoke commending him on his ministry. Father Olivarez seems always to be present with the poor, celebrating mass with the United Farm Workers, speaking on behalf of the people of Central America, announcing that his congregation is a Sanctuary for Central American refugees. Fr. Olivarez briefly thanked the people who had spoken and expressed his gratitude for the movements of the poor which had brought him the opportunities, he said, for the conversions of his life. Fr. Luis has made the poor a priority in his life and has been blessed by them.

But even these steps are not enough for the institutional Church. Chris Hartmire emphasizes that the Church "needs to put a priority on these folks, it needs to set aside part of its flesh and blood to be with them. The Church needs to say, 'These movements of poor people are important to us,' and not give them grants but release somebody or somebodies from our midst to work with them, knowing that it is going to have an impact on us. We're going to have to own that person, and it will be very hard for us to say to that person, 'We don't understand what you mean, and we won't do what the people need.'

It seems to me that all other forms of help are not worthy of us, or worthy of people who are struggling to do something right. Everything else keeps us in the position of being able to turn it on and off, or to decide yes or no, or the budget is too tight this year. Churches had a terrible time with us. They just couldn't turn off the spigot. It was too hard, because we were real people that they knew and they had sent . . . And since we weren't drunk or weren't maladministering the resources or sleeping with farm workers on the side, it was real hard for them to say no to us.[7]

The desperation of dispossessed people and their appeals for help come to us every day. The need of the Church, however, is more subtle. Even when church bodies are being prophetic: speaking to Congress about our wrong-headed policy in Central America; calling on the U.S. government to withdraw support for apartheid in South Africa. And even when Church leaders are preaching about the way to peace and the need for justice. Whatever the institutions of the Church choose to do or not do, every person, member, pastor, or church executive—every one of us has responsibility for our own conversions.

As congregations and individuals, we need, time and again, to be turned off the paved highway marked "Status Quo." We need to turn on to the rutted dirt byways with no markings. The only way we know we're on the right road is that all the poor people are on it. They're walking. And they greet us on the road and tell us how glad they are we've finally come. And they give us a little of their burdens to carry.

It's not easy like the highway. We have to leave the comfort of our car and proceed on foot. We get tired helping to carry the burdens of others. But, astonishingly, the load never feels as heavy as it looks. We are heartened to hear that if we walk long enough we will all reach a beautiful city where there's free board and room for everyone. And in the meantime, the homeless and the hungry share what they have with us. And there's enough.

Appendix

Following is information on abbreviations and name changes for the United Farm Workers Union and for the National Farm Worker Ministry.

National Farm Workers Association (NFWA) had its organizing convention in Fresno, California in the Fall of 1962 under the leadership of Cesar Chavez.

Agricultural Workers Organizing Committee, AFL-CIO (AWOC) went on strike in September 1965 against certain Delano grape growers. NFWA voted to join the strike.

August 1966 NFWA and AWOC merged into United Farm Workers Organizing Committee, AFL-CIO (UFWOC), with Cesar Chavez as Director.

February 1972 UFWOC received charter from the AFL-CIO and became United Farm Workers Union (UFW).

The California Migrant Ministry was dissolved and all staff and resources were transferred to the new National Farm Worker Ministry in January 1972. This was a response to the UFW's need for an agency suitable for giving national Church leadership in support of national boycotts and organizing efforts in several states. There was extensive debate about what to call the new organization. National Migrant Ministry seemed to limit it to farm workers who were still migrating. However, many farm workers knew and trusted "The Migrant Ministry." That name has continued in use and has been shortened by UFW people to "The Ministry."

Notes

CHAPTER 1

1. Interview with Rev. John R. Moyer, New York City, March 28, 1985.
2. "California Migrant Ministry Newsletter" Vol.2, No.1, Spring 1969, p.3.
3. Telephone interview with Rev. Douglas Still.
4. Rev. Wayne C. Hartmire, "The Church and the Emerging Farm Worker Movement," National Farm Worker Ministry, Los Angeles, 1967, p.13.
5. Ibid.,p.10.
6. Ibid., p.12.
7. Interview with Dr. Richard Norberg, San Mateo, Calif., February 27, 1985.
8. A presbytery is the smallest local judicatory in the Presbyterian Church. Clergy are ordained by their home presbytery and hold membership in a presbytery, usually the one in which they are working.
9. Interview with Rev. Jim Drake, San Antonio, Texas, March 21, 1985.
10. Hartmire, "Emerging Farm Worker Movement," p.13.
11. Drake interview.
12. Hartmire, "Emerging Farm Worker Movement," p.14.
13. Drake interview.
14. Hartmire, "Emerging Farm Worker Movement," p.14.
15. Norberg interview.
16. Hartmire, "Emerging Farm Worker Movement," p.15.
17. The rose strike did not result in a contract or any permanent gains.
18. Hartmire, "Emerging Farm Worker Movement," pp.5–7.
19. Ibid., p.9.

20. Ibid., p.14.
21. Interview with Rev. Wayne C. Hartmire, La Paz, October 25, 1984.
22. Hartmire, "Emerging Farm Worker Movement," pp.16–17.

CHAPTER 2

1. Hartmire, "Emerging Farm Worker Movement," p.19.
2. Ibid.
3. Ibid.
4. Interview with Rev. Charles McLain in Oakland, Calif., February 25, 1985.
5. Jacques E. Levy, *Cesar Chavez: Autobiography of la Causa.* W.W. Norton, 1975, p.228.
6. Ibid.
7. Mark Day, *Forty Acres, Cesar Chavez and the Farm Workers,* p.55.
8. Ibid.
9. Levy,*Cesar Chavez*, p.193.
10. Levy, *Cesar Chavez*, quote from Chavez, p.266.
11. *El Malcriado*, 3/3/66, p.4.
12. Drake interview.
13. Interview with Dr. Richard Norberg, San Mateo, Calif., February 27, 1985.
14. Interview with Fr. Eugene Boyle, Palo Alto, Calif., March 1, 1985.
15. Interview with Dr. Loris Coletta, Rolling Hills Estates, Calif., August 14, 1985.
16. p.45.
17. Levy, *Cesar Chavez*, p.275.
18. Ibid.
19. Ibid.
20. Levy, *Cesar Chavez*, p.46.
21. Levy, *Cesar Chavez*, p.277ff.
22. pp.47–48.
23. Levy, *Cesar Chavez*, p.301.
24. p.88.
25. Quoted in Levy, *Cesar Chavez*, p. 485.
26. "Minutes, Ninth General Synod—Including Addresses", St. Louis, Missouri, June 22-26, 1973, including Synod tape of proceedings related to Coachella Delegation.
27. Moyer interview.
28. Synod tape.

29. Norberg interview.
30. Moyer interview.
31. Levy, *Cesar Chavez*, p.495.
32. Interview with Rose Cecilia Harrington, CSJ, Los Angeles, November 15, 1985.
33. Boyle interview.
34. Levy, *Cesar Chavez*, p.505.
35. p.503.
36. Interview with Jack Ahern, San Francisco, February 27, 1985.

CHAPTER 3

1. From speech by Rabbi Sanford Ragin at World Food Day Conference, Los Angeles, Fall 1984.
2. Drake interview.
3. Interview with Rev. August Vandenbosche, Atlanta, Georgia, March 27, 1985.
4. Interview with Marilyn Schafer, Los Angeles, November 26, 1985.
5. Interview with Dr. Ralph Kennedy, Santa Fe Springs, Calif., November 25, 1985.
6. Interview with Jean Giordano, Corona del Mar, Calif., August 14, 1985.
7. Interview with Lynn Ransford, Los Angeles, July 24, 1985.
8. Interview with Jessica Govea, Inglewood, Calif., December 5, 1985.
9. Interview with Dr. James Stewart, Los Angeles, July 30, 1985.
10. Interview with Adria Raquel Venegas Lawson, Oxnard, April 2, 1985.
11. Interview with Dr. G. Wooden Garvin, Pasadena, Calif., June 19, 1985.
12. Interview with LeRoy Chatfield, Sacramento, Calif., February 28, 1985.
13. Hartmire interview.
14. Interview with Fred Ross, San Anselmo, Calif., February 26, 1985.

CHAPTER 4

1. Interview with Cesar Chavez at La Paz, U.F.W. Headquarters, by Pat Hoffman for *Sojourners* magazine, 1977.
2. Hartmire's notes to the author.

3. Farm labor was already successfully organized in Hawaii.
4. Interview with religious woman who asked for anonymity to protect her family.
5. Interview with Marilyn Rudy, CSJ, in Los Angeles, June 18, 1985.
6. Interview with Rev. Karl Irvin, Oakland, Calif., February 12, 1986.
7. Interview with Allan Grant, San Joaquin Valley, March 18, 1986.
8. p.20.
9. Interview with Jessie de la Cruz, Fresno, Calif., March 17, 1986.
10. Interview with Rev. Charles McLain, Oakland, February 12, 1986.
11. Anonymous interview.
12. p.5.
13. Unpublished correspondence to *Monday Morning*, February 20, 1986.
14. Private correspondence.
15. In 1960 there was a strong lobbying attempt by churches and other groups to get a minimum wage law for farm workers in California of seventy cents an hour. Governor Edmund G. Brown supported the legislation but it was defeated by the legislature. Subsequently the Industrial Welfare Commission ruled on a minimum wage covering women and adolescents. Men were not included in the regulation. The result was that growers did not hire women and teenagers that year. Their exclusion from employment put terrible burdens on families dependent on earnings from all those in the family able to work. Supporters of the minimum wage simply didn't have the power to make useful change.
16. Telephone interview with Rev. Eugene Boutilier, July 17, 1985.
17. Interview with Rev. Winthrop B. Yinger, Oakland, March 30, 1986.
18. Interviews with Rev. William Dew and Mitzi Dew, Alamo, Calif., March 20, 1986.

CHAPTER 5

1. Interview with Rev. Wayne C. Hartmire, La Paz, June 16, 1985.
2. Wayne C. Hartmire, "The Plight of Seasonal Farm Workers," *Christianity and Crisis*, October 4, 1965, p.2 of reprint.
3. Hartmire, "United Farm Workers: Reflections on the Church's Ministry," *Migration Today*, Number 20, 1981, p.2.
4. From Hartmire's photocopied, annotated quotes from Bonhoeffer.
5. Hartmire's description.

6. Hartmire's quotes from Bonhoeffer.
7. Dr. Dan W. Dodson, "Does Community Organizing Process Preserve and Enhance the Dignity and Work of the Individual?", published by Dept. of Publications, NCCC, 1965.
8. Hartmire, "Emerging Farm Worker Movement," p.34.
9. October 1984 interview with Hartmire.
10. Interview with Dr. Clifford Crummey, Oakland, February 26, 1985.
11. Norberg interview.
12. Ibid.
13. Synanon, a drug rehabilitation program, used "the Game," in which participants met regularly to say exactly what they thought about each other. There were to be no recriminations beyond the session. The UFW adopted "the Game" and used it for a while at La Paz, UFW headquarters. Hartmire noted that Jim Drake never directly participated in "the Game."
14. Drake interview.
15. Interview with Monsignor George Higgins, Washington, D.C., March 29, 1985.
16. "If we had taken only a few steps away from the movement, it would be too far. Why? Because an important part of our own energy and stamina for the long haul comes from the urgency and vitality of the movement . . . Because we would lose that location, that position in the movement which enables us to lead supporters in the direction that makes sense to farm workers' struggle . . . Because we would no longer be naturally there for celebrating the Eucharist, burying the dead, comforting the sick . . . Because we would lose our day-to-day influence in the movement . . . And finally and most importantly because we would be less present with our human energy and therefore less useful to a struggle that needs all the strength it can get." Chris Hartmire, "United Farm Workers: Reflections on the Church's Ministry," *Migration Today*, Number 28, 1981.
17. "National Farm Worker Ministry Newsletter," Spring 1986.

CHAPTER 6

1. Interview with Cesar Chavez, La Paz, June 16, 1985.
2. Interview with Mark Day, Los Angeles, June 4, 1985.

3. Telephone interview with Rev. Elizabeth Kratz, June 6, 1986.
4. Rudy interview.
5. Interview with Katrina Carter, Santa Monica, Calif., May 31, 1986.
6. Interview with Rev. Howard Matson, Carmel Valley, Calif., October 11, 1985.
7. Hartmire 1984 interview.

Bibliography

BOOKS

Day, Mark, *Forty Acres: Cesar Chavez and the Farm Workers*, New York, Praeger, 1971.

Levy, Jacques E., *Cesar Chavez: Autobiography of la Causa*, New York, W.W. Norton, 1975.

ARTICLES

El Malcriado. Published by the United Farm Workers, Keene, California. (Articles referred to were published by the UFW in Delano, California.)

Grant, Allan. "California Grapes and the Boycott, the Growers' Side of the Story." *Presbyterian Life*. December 1, 1968.

"Harvester." California Migrant Ministry Newsletters. On file at National Farm Worker Ministry (NFWM), 111A Fairmount, Oakland, CA 94611.

Hartmire, Wayne C. "The Church and the Emerging Farm Worker's Movement." Los Angeles, California Migrant Ministry, 1967. On file at N.F.W.M.

_____. "The Plight of Seasonal Farm Workers." *Christianity and Crisis*, October 4, 1965.

_____. "United Farm Workers: Reflections on the Church's Ministry." *Migration Today*, Number 28, 1981.

Hogue, James L.. "Protection for the Agricultural Worker." *Monday Morning*. February 9, 1970. Published by The United Presbyterian Church (USA).

ADDRESSES, PROCEEDINGS,
AND UNPUBLISHED MATERIALS

Bennett, Dr. John C. "The Church and Power Conflicts." Address available from files of NFWM, 111A Fairmount, Oakland, California 94611.

Hartmire, Wayne C. Photocopied and annotated quotes from Bonhoeffer. Personal papers.

_____. Unpublished correspondence related to conflict in the Church over support for the United Farm Workers.

"Minutes, Ninth General Synod—Including Addresses, St. Louis, Missouri, June 22-26, 1973." United Church of Christ, 132 W. 31st Street, New York, New York 10001. Tape recording of proceedings, events in Coachella and St. Louis related to delegation from Ninth General Synod of United Church of Christ to Coachella. Available from the United Church of Christ.

Ragin, Rabbi Sanford. Speech before Southern California Interfaith Hunger Coalition's World Food Day Conference. Los Angeles, Fall 1984.

INTERVIEWS

The following interviews were conducted by Pat Hoffman and were taped unless it is noted that they were not. Tapes and transcripts are not available to the general public.

Anonymous. With religious woman. 4/4/86.

Ahern, Jack. San Francisco, 2/27/85.

Boutilier, Rev. Eugene. Telephone interview. Los Angeles, 7/17/85.

Boyle, Fr. Eugene. Palo Alto, California, 3/1/85.

Carter, Katrina. Santa Monica, 5/31/86.

Carter, Rev. Lawrence. Santa Monica, 5/31/86.

Chatfield, LeRoy. Sacramento, 2/27/85.

Chavez, Cesar. Keene, California, 6/16/85 and an earlier interview in Fall 1977 for *Sojourners'* magazine.

Cohen, Jerome. Carmel, California 3/1/85 and 3/2/85.

Coletta, Dr. Loris, Rolling Hills Estates, California, 8/14/86.

Crummey, Rev. Clifford. Oakland, 2/26/85.

Day, Mark. Los Angeles, 6/4/85.

De la Cruz, Jessie. Fresno, 3/17/86.

Dew, Mitzi. Alamo, California, 3/5/86.

Dew, Rev. William. Alamo, California, 3/5/86.

Drake, Rev. Jim. San Antonio, Texas, 3/21/85.

Ganz, Marshall. Salinas, California, 3/1/85.

Garvin, Dr. G. Wooden. Pasadena, California, 6/19/85.

Giordano, Jean. Corona del Mar, California, 8/14/85.

Goble, Dorothy. San Jose, California, 10/10/85.

Govea, Jessica. Inglewood, California, 12/5/85.

Grant, Allan. Chowchilla, California, 3/18/86.

Harrington, Sr. Rose Cecilia. Los Angeles, 11/15/85.

Hartmire, Rev. Wayne C. Keene, California, 10/25/84, 6/16/85, and communications by telephone and correspondence.

Hernandez, Lydia. Atlanta, Georgia, 3/28/85.

Higgins, Monsignor George. Washington, D.C., 3/29/85.

Irvin, Rev. Karl. Oakland, 2/12/86.

Irvin, Ethelyn. Oakland, 2/12/86.

Kratz, Rev. Elizabeth. Telephone interview, 6/16/86.

Kennedy, Dr. Ralph. Santa Fe Springs, California, 11/25/85.

Lawson, Adria Raquel Venegas. Oxnard, California, 4/2/85.

Lawson, Karl. Oxnard, California, 4/2/85.

McCoy, Fr. Alan. Santa Barbara, California, 4/2/85.

McLain, Rev. Charles. Oakland, 2/12/86.

Magana, Maria Saludado. Lakeside, California, 4/4/86.

Matson, Rev. Howard. Carmel Valley, California, 10/11/85.

Matson, Rosemary. Carmel Valley, California, 10/11/85.

Moyer, Rev. John C.. Inglewood, California, 12/3/85.

Moyer, Rev. John R.. New York City, New York, 3/28/85.

Norberg, Dr. Richard. San Mateo, California, 2/27/85.

Press, Rev. Walter. San Rafael, California, 2/26/85.

Ransford, Lynn. Los Angeles, California, 7/24/85.

Ross, Fred. San Anselmo, California, 2/26/85.

Rudy, Sr. Marilyn. Los Angeles, 6/18/85.

Schafer, Marilyn. Los Angeles, 11/26/85.

Stewart, Dr. James. Los Angeles, 7/30/85.

Still, Rev. Douglas. Telephone interview, 1985.

Vandenbosche, Rev. August. Atlanta, Georgia, 3/27/85.

Welch, Gertrude. San Jose, California, 10/10/85.

Yinger, Rev. Winthrop B., Oakland, 3/20/86.

Index

Christian Brothers (religious order): 23, 72
Christian Brothers (winery): 39
Church Women United: ix, 60, 118, 130. See also United Church Women
Civil Rights Movement: 55, 80, 81
Clergy, on the picket line: Boutilier, Rev. Eugene, 90-91; McLain, Rev. Charles, 32-33; Yinger, Rev. Winthrop, 92
CMM. See California Migrant Ministry
Coachella Valley: 18, 45, 46, 47-49, 79, 132; Strike in, 6, 47
Coachella, California: 19, 44, 48
Coca Cola: 60
Cohen, Ann: 49
Cohen, Jerome ("Jerry"): 29, 42, 52
Coletta, Loris: 37, 38
Collins, Rev. Dean: 12
Commission on Social Justice: 53
Community development: 18
Community organization/organizing: 12, 13, 27, 28, 99, 100, 112, 122
Community Service Organization (CSO): 13, 66, 84
Conflict Phobia: 105
Congregational Church: 17, 21, 92; First, of Fresno, 90, see also United Church of Christ
Council of Women for Home Missions: 8
Crummey, Rev. Clifford: 109, 132
CSO. See Community Service Organization

Daifullah, Nagi: 53
Day Care Centers: 8
Day, Dorothy: 50
Day, Mark: 41, 123-124; *Forty Acres*, 33, 40, 43, 44
De la Cruz, Arnold: 85
De la Cruz, Jessie: 85-86, 128

De la Cruz, Juan: 53
De la Cruz, Roberto ("Bobby"): 70, 73
De Santiana, Julio: *Towards A Church of the Poor*, 133
Delano Ministerial Association: 33
Delano, California: Cesar Chavez to, 24, 84
Dew, Mitzi: 95
Dew, Rev. William: 94-95
DiGiorgio: 63, 107, 110; Boycott against, 73; Corporation, 39
Diocese: Roman Catholic; of Fresno, 36; of Orange, 62; of San Francisco, 37
Disciples of Christ: 81, 124
Dispoto, Bruno: 33
Division of Home Missions: 12
Donnelly, Bishop: 45. See also Bishops Committee
Dow Chemical Company, boycott of: 30
Drake, Rev. Jim: x, 18-21, 22, 23, 25, 27, 35-36, 43, 58, 71, 78, 112-113, 115-116, 132
Drake, Susan: 21
Drydyk, Sr. Pat: 118
Dunn, Sr. Clare: 125

East Harlem: 16
Ecumenism: 132-133
Eichner, Jane (Mrs. Wayne C. Hartmire): 15
El Malcriado: 20, 22, 35, 63
Empowerment: 1, 98, 99, 105, 107, 121, 124, 126; Self-determination, 13, 15, 16, 19, 20, 119
Episcopal Diocese of San Joaquin: 78
Europe: 6
Evangelical and Reform Church: 17
Eyster, Rev. Fred: ix

Farm Labor Organizing Committee (FLOC): 118, 131

About the Author

Pat Hoffman has been an activist on social justice issues. She worked as a church organizer with the National Farm Worker Ministry during the time examined in this book. She later worked with the Southern California Interfaith Hunger Coalition. For five years she was administrator and fund developer for Community Counseling Service in Los Angeles, helping to make available psychological services for poor blacks, Hispanics and others in that city. She has written numerous articles related to her areas of work.

She has been involved with U.S. policy in Central America and traveled to Nicaragua. Her volunteer work for justice has generally been in the setting of the ecumenical church. She is a member of a union congregation, United University Church in Los Angeles, a Presbyterian/Methodist congregation. Ms. Hoffman is a Presbyterian elder.

She is married to a psychologist who is also a Presbyterian clergyman, Cecil Hoffman. They have three adult children. The Hoffmans live in the Los Angeles area.

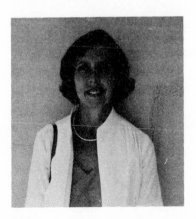

TO ORDER THIS BOOK

Send $8.95 plus $1.25 for shipping to:

Wallace Press
P.O. Box 83850
Los Angeles, CA 90083

(In California add 58 cents tax for each book.)